the hand-stitched surface

LYNN KRAWCZYK

Slow Stitching
and Mixed-Media
Techniques for
Fabric and Paper

Creative Publishing
international

Quarto is the authority on a wide range of topics.

Quarto educates, entertains and enriches the lives of
our readers—enthusiasts and lovers of hands-on living.

www.QuartoKnows.com

First published in the United States of America
in 2017 by Creative Publishing international, an
imprint of Quarto Publishing Group USA Inc.
400 First Avenue North, Suite 400
Minneapolis, MN 55401

1-800-328-3895

QuartoKnows.com

Visit our blogs at QuartoKnows.com

Library of Congress Cataloging-in-Publication Data

Names: Krawczyk, Lynn, author.
Title: The hand-stitched surface : slow stitching and
mixed-media techniques
  for fabric and paper / Lynn Krawczyk.
Description: Beverly : Creative Publishing int'l, 2017.
Identifiers: LCCN 2016047834 | ISBN
9781589239425 (paperback)
Subjects: LCSH: Stitches (Sewing) | Paper work--Pat-
terns. | Textile
  crafts--Patterns. | BISAC: CRAFTS & HOBBIES /
Needlework / General. |
  CRAFTS & HOBBIES / Needlework / Embroidery.
Classification: LCC TT715 .K73 2017 | DDC 746--dc23
LC record available at https://lccn.loc.
gov/2016047834

Design: Timothy Samara

Photography: Lynn Krawczyk

Printed in China

This book is for every artist who
has used thread and needle to bare
their creative soul.

Contents

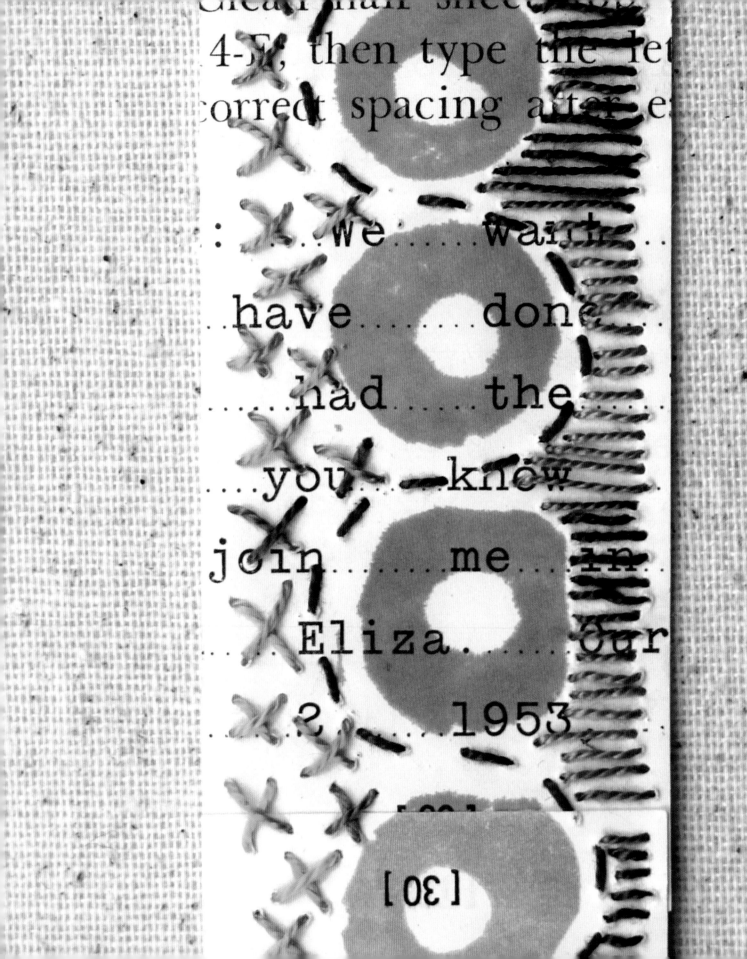

Preface

I wrote this book in fifteen minutes. No, really, I did.

Okay, okay. *Several* fifteen-minute time blocks. Still, it's not an endeavor that required me to lock myself away in a remote cabin for six months to accomplish.

This is one of many reasons why I love hand stitching. It's the type of thing that you can toss in your bag to work on in those spare moments when you would otherwise go mad waiting for an appointment or to make a long trip feel more bearable. Aside from its magical, sanity-saving abilities, hand stitching has a long history that I feel a personal responsibility to keep alive as much as possible.

There is something sacred about performing the same motions and stitches that have been created for centuries by other stitchers. And because historically this art form has been a woman's domain, has often been overlooked.

While the speed of your hand stitching will likely pick up the more practiced you become, it's not something that can be rushed. It's slow and methodical, and in a world where we are connected to anyone and anywhere on the globe, I consider it a necessity to be able to remove myself completely. This art form does not require any kind of technology—it's totally off the grid.

I consider hand stitching a kind of universal language. Every culture has its own special version that reflects its beliefs and unique way of seeing the world. From kantha embroidery in India to sashiko in Japan and folk embroidery in Poland, hand stitching has a quiet history that is very deep and sacred.

My hope for you, my fellow hand stitcher, is that this book will inspire you to explore this art form and integrate it into your life the way I have. I can't tell you the pleasure and peace it has given me. I enjoy making art in many different forms—art quilts, handmade books, paintings, wearable art. If there is a place I can park some hand stitching, I immediately reach for the needle and threads. No matter what art form dominates your imagination, hand stitching has a place if only you're willing to open your heart and mind to it.

What Is "Slow Stitching"?

I remember the world before the internet. I remember
when answering machines with tapes were an incredible
technological advance and how the neighbors waited
on the front porch for the cable rep who was signing people
up because it was the first time such a thing existed.

I remember summer days of bike riding and book reading
and not a single electronic screen sitting before me.
I remember going to the library and smelling the dust on
the pages and digging through the card catalog to find
what I wanted. I remember when recipes were handed
down on handwritten index cards.

And I remember sitting on the front porch of my childhood
home, nodding to neighbors as they walked to the corner
store for ice cream.

This was when the world moved at a slower pace, and
while I am in no way dogging technology (I use a lot of it
myself and really enjoy it), I wonder if the world would
be a little bit of a better place if it   could   just
– –

learn   t o

S L O W   D O W N   .

Hand stitching leading to world peace is a stretch, but my point is that what we build in our own personal worlds feeds out into everything else. "Slow stitching" is about being present, about living fully in the moment instead of rushing just to get things done and tick them off the list.

When you first hear the phrase "slow stitching," you may be tempted to think of a woman sitting in her chair, toiling at her stitching project with painfully slow motion–style movements.

Not the case at all.

While it does refer to the speed at which we work, "slow stitching" is rooted in the idea that your project takes on a whole new layer of meaning when you choose to spend more time with it. This creates a bond between you and your work that shows in the final product.

It also creates your history in a unique form of record keeping. Items that you created with your own two hands can be passed from family member to family member over the years.

Slow stitching is all about taking time and allowing yourself that special space to create and to keep this incredible art form thriving.

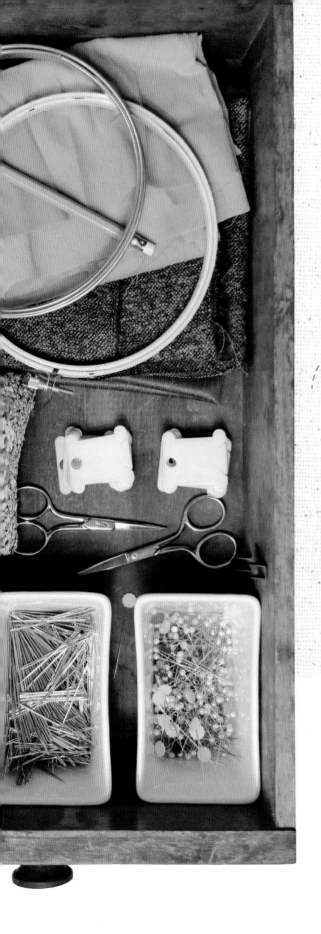

HAND-STITCHING ESSENTIALS

One of the nice things about hand stitching is that all of the materials and tools are portable. You can toss every single thing you need to hand stitch a project into a tote bag and you're an instant mobile art studio. Your stitching essentials toolbox is, for the most part, fairly basic.

Basic Tool Kit

You'll need thread, needles, and embroidery scissors for any stitching project, whether you're working on fabric or paper. The most essential of these—thread and needles—are discussed on the following pages. The particular materials and tools you'll need for stitching on fabric or on paper are described later in this chapter.

Your basic toolkit can include other items such as a thimble, needle threader, and sewing box. You'll find that some hand stitchers use tools that you don't particularly care for. (I have personally never been able to warm up to using a thimble.) So while it's impossible to hand stitch without some items, others will depend solely on personal preference.

Thread

Thread is by far the most fun tool in your arsenal. Solid or variegated colors, cotton or silk or wool, floss or perle twist, thin or heavy—you will never be bored when choosing thread for your projects!

I have very few allegiances when it comes to thread. Basically, if I can thread it through a needle, I'll stitch with it. The best recommendation I can give for thread is this—use the best quality you can afford and the kind you love. If you love working with it, it will show in your project.

A stitch made with cotton floss is affected by the number of strands used. From left to right: stitches made with a single strand to all six strands.

Floss

Floss consists of six individual strands of lightweight thread that can be separated. The beauty of this type of thread is that you can choose how heavy you want your stitch to appear by using more or fewer strands.

I recommend that you always separate the strands, no matter how many you're using. Even if you plan to use all six strands at one time, pull them apart first and thread together as a group. Why bother doing this? Because separating the strands takes the twist out of them. You'll get much fluffier stitches by doing this.

Here's how you separate out a stand of floss.

1

Cut a length of thread no more than 18" (45.6 cm) long.

2

Loosely hold one end between your forefinger and thumb.

3

Grab the end of one strand and slowly begin pulling. The thread will begin to bunch, but keep pulling. The single strand will come free.

4

Straighten out the remaining strands and repeat for as many strands as you want to use.

Perle cotton

This is a two-ply thread that cannot be divided like cotton floss. It comes in various weights, with the smallest number equaling the heaviest thread.

Wool thread

This thread has a slight fuzz to it. You most often find it in thinner weights. Use more than one strand for a heavier stitch.

Sashiko thread

This is a twisted nondivisible cotton thread. It has a weight a little heavier than a perle size 5, but where it differs is that it has a matte finish, making it unique.

Linen thread

This thread is stiffer than the others we've discussed, and it creates a thinner line.

Silk thread

This kind of thread comes in stranded and perle forms. Its sheen is incredibly addictive, and it's incredibly easy to stitch with.

Perle cotton in the most common sizes (from left to right): 5, 8, and 12.

A variety of threads (from left to right): wool, cotton sashiko, linen, and silk perle.

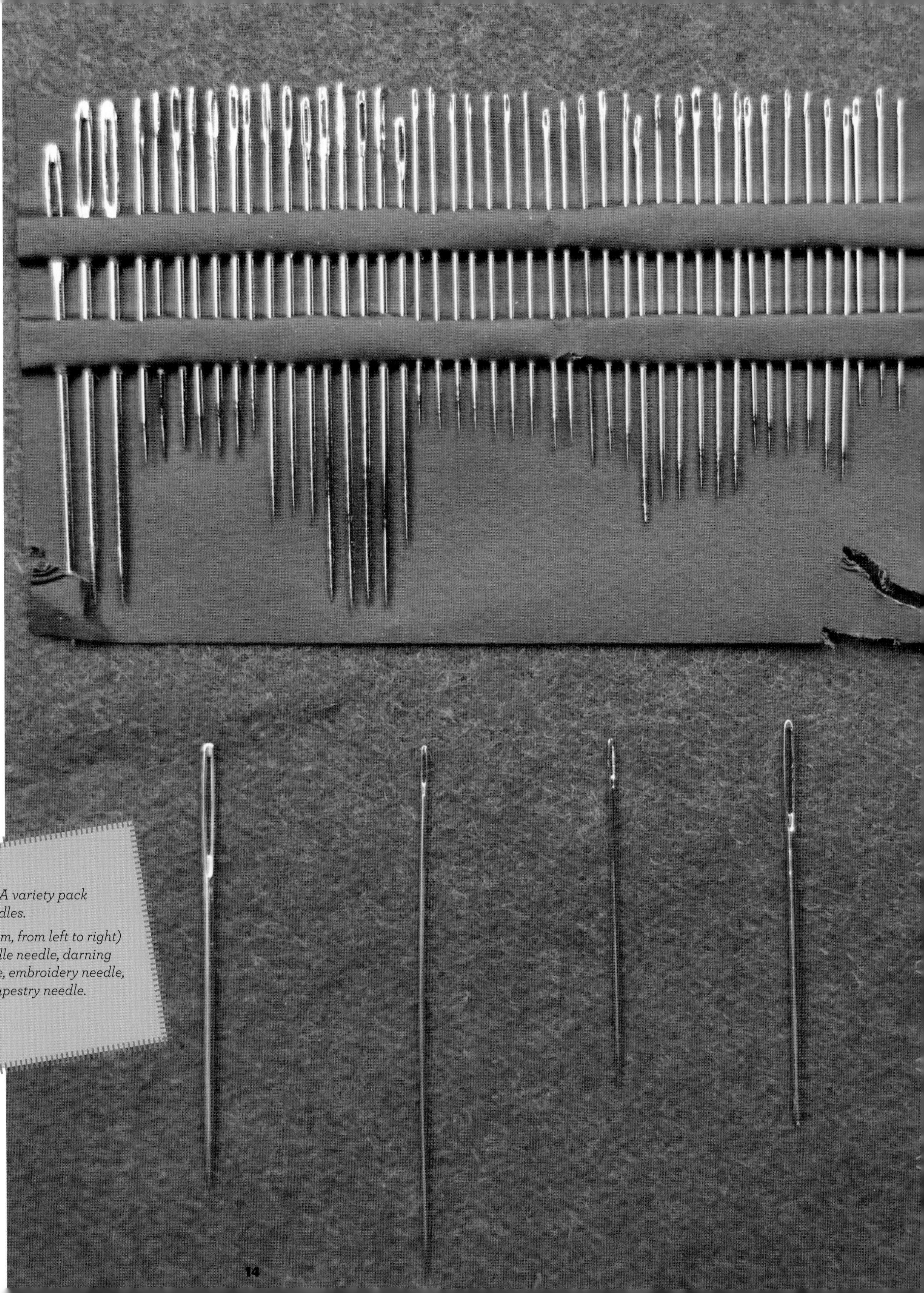

(Top) A variety pack
of needles.

(Bottom, from left to right)
Chenille needle, darning
needle, embroidery needle,
and tapestry needle.

Needles

The needle you choose for your project is important—choose one too thin and you'll stress the thread; choose one too large and the hole it makes will remain visible after the thread is pulled through.

Here are some of the most common ones. Note that, like thread, the lower the number designated on a needle size, the thicker it is.

Embroidery needles

These are just what they sound like—needles made for hand stitching. They work better for thinner weight threads. I use size 5—most often because it's an in-between size. In a size 5, there's very little flair between the eye of the needle and the shank, so it's a master at not leaving evidence of a hole behind.

Chenille needles

These are for heavier threads, like perle weights. They work really well for thicker fabrics and projects with several layers.

Tapestry needles

These are similar to chenille needles except that their tip is blunt instead of sharp. These needles work well for weaving projects.

Using a Needle Book

A needle book isn't something you have to have, but it sure is handy. It does exactly what it implies—it holds all your needles in one place until you're ready to use them. I can't tell you how many packs of needles I bought (and lost) and rebought (and lost again) because I wasn't using a needle book. I'd stick them in projects or fabric scraps, always thinking I'd remember where to find them. I didn't. So I strongly recommend getting or making one of these. I've included a project for making your very own needle book (see page 72) so you can create a custom needle book to your liking!

Tools and Tips for Stitching on Fabric

Here's a rundown of what you'll need—and need to know—when hand stitching on fabric.

Fabrics

I use many different types of fabric for the projects in this book. All have endeared themselves to me for one reason or another. Most of the time, I work with heavier to medium-weight fabric. Since I don't like working with an embroidery hoop (see *Tools,* on the following spread), those weights add stability to my project.

Below is a brief description of each fabric and why I like it. This is by no means a comprehensive list of what kinds of fabric you can stitch on. If you have a fabric that you just adore that isn't discussed here, then use it!

100 percent quilting-weight cotton

This is the most common cotton-weight fabric you'll find in craft stores. It can range from a very dense weave to lightweight and thinner. I lean more toward solid-color fabric for my hand-stitched projects. I love that it puts the thread and stitches front and center.

Linen

This too is a versatile fabric, and it comes in many weaves and weights. The thing I love most about linen is that the weave is so obvious. Being able to see the weave adds to the beauty of the stitched fabric. Linen comes in many different blends and colors. I lean more toward natural and white colors, but it's not impossible to find linen in vibrant colors.

Raw silk

I have a deep affection for raw silk. The texture of it makes me swoon. It's a heavier weight than many of the silks that are used for scarves but still has a wonderful drape. I also love its natural color, a lovely cream color that has such warmth to it.

Osnaburg

This is a coarser cotton fabric that I've only ever encountered as a natural color. I like it because the weave has flecks in it, which lends interesting visual texture.

Felt

I love both the stability and the pliability of felt. On thicker felt, the stitches sink ever so slightly into it and feel more integrated. I love that! I use both acrylic felt and a wool felt blend. I find the wool felt blend easier to work with than 100 percent wool felt, which can be quite dense depending on how it's made. Felt comes in a huge array of colors and is easy to find in both small sheets and yardage. Heathered felt has specks of gray or beige in it to create a more complex color. This can add some beautiful depth to a project. I also use felt to add more stability to a project. A layer of felt adds enough thickness so that the project has some structure and it's easier to control the tension.

Some stitching fabric (from top to bottom): quilting cotton, linen, 100 percent wool felt, raw silk, felt wool/rayon blend, and osnaburg.

Tools

Supplement your basic tool kit with these essential fabric, stitching supplies.

(Clockwise from left): A roll of water-soluble stabilizer, transfer paper, and an embroidery hoop.

Embroidery scissors

These are a must. These are small scissors that help you get into small places and snip specific threads. Standard-size scissors can be clunky and you run the risk of accidentally cutting a hole in the project (ask me how I know).

Embroidery hoops

Embroidery hoops are a wonderful support aid for hand stitching. They consist of two hoops. You place your project over the top of the inner hoop, place the outer hoop over that, and tighten the screw to create tension on the fabric. It's important not to stretch the fabric too much or you can cause distortions or permanent stretching that can't be removed. (Cotton, especially, is susceptible to this.) It's also a good idea to remove your project from the hoop whenever you're done with a work session. This will prevent the hoop from making permanent marks on the fabric. You can add a layer of defense against hoop marks by wrapping the inner hoop with a strip of fabric. This acts as a buffer between the hoop and your fabric.

I'll be totally honest with you—I'm not a fan of embroidery hoops, and I rarely use them. Part of me believes that I learned good control over my tension by ignoring them. I practiced on single layers of fabric until I was able to do a running stitch without creating any puckers in the textile. This is not to say you shouldn't use a hoop if you like it; rather, if you find them uncomfortable to work with, you can skip them and still achieve wonderful results.

Pins

The best advice I can give about pins is this—use ones that are appropriate to the weight of the fabric you're working on and use ones with flat heads. Pins have different-size diameters, so if your fabric is delicate, you can leave holes in it if you use a pin that is too large. Quilting pins have flat heads, which keep them from distorting the fabric while they're holding your project together.

Pincushion

Pincushions serve a very utilitarian purpose—they're a place to park your needles and your pins so you don't end up stepping on them. That doesn't mean they can't be fun! Whether you choose a quirky vintage cushion that's seen the work of several stitchers or a brand-new one from the craft store, this item will see a lot of action during your work time.

Marking pens

Marking pens let you draw a pattern onto fabric for stitching. They come in two varieties—chalk and water-soluble marker. The chalk often gets rubbed off during stitching, or it can be removed using a damp cloth. Chalk works really well on darker fabric. Water-soluble markers produce a much more pronounced outline and won't rub off from handling.

It can only be removed through washing or blotting with a wet towel. However, it's extremely important to test both the fabric and the thread when using a water-soluble marker. Although dyers make every effort to ensure their colors won't bleed, better safe than sorry. This applies to both chalk and marker marking.

Transfer paper

This paper accomplishes the same thing as using a chalk marker. The advantage is that you can trace over a design you've already created rather than drawing freehand onto the fabric. My preferred brand is Transdoodle from Mistyfuse, but there are other brands on the market that also work well.

Water-soluble stabilizer

This stuff is like magic. It's a type of plastic that is extremely easy to stitch through. Simply draw the design you want to stitch onto the stabilizer, place over the fabric, and stitch away. A soak in warm water makes it disappear, and you're left with just fabric and thread.

Fabric-Stitching Tips

I'd like to share this round-up of advice and guidance that's based on the wisdom of my personal experience (both good and bad).

—

Test thread for colorfastness before you start stitching. Although thread companies make every effort to ensure their colors won't bleed, it does happen. I lay a few short strands of thread across a white piece of fabric, wet it, then fold it over on itself and rub it together to see if any dye transfers. You'll see fairly quickly whether the thread could cause any unwanted blotches on your project.

—

Work with strands of thread that are no longer than 18" (45.6 cm). I strongly, strongly, strongly (did I say strongly?) recommend this. Anything beyond this length is sure to lead to knots and frustration. Plus, using this length reduces the number of times the thread gets pulled through the project, so it won't show any signs of stress or fraying.

—

When creating large stitches, you run the risk of them snagging because they're looser. Add a small tack stitch somewhere in the stitch that can be hidden to give it the stability it needs.

—

When straight stitching around a curve, take smaller stitches. This helps maintain the curved appearance of the stitching patterns.

—

Add stitches with thinner thread in a contrasting color along finished stitch patterns to create a sense of depth and visual interest.

—

When you travel long distances between stitches, sometimes you end up with a longer thread on the back that could get snagged and wreck the stitches on the front by pulling them too tight. There are two ways you can secure long thread travelers:

① If you're stitching on a single layer of fabric or on paper, weave the thread under other stitches to keep it secure.

② If you're working on more than one layer of fabric, you can take a stitch or two through the back fabric to get to the new location where you will continue stitching.

—

I have two ways that I like to secure threads when I come to the end of stitching with them:

① If you're working on multiple layers of fabric, take a couple of small stitches through the back fabric and snip the thread.

② If you're working on a single layer of fabric, pass the thread underneath the previous stitch, pull the thread until it becomes a loop, and pass the needle through that. Repeat one more time to create a knot.

Creating a Mobile Stitch Studio

The beauty of hand stitching is that you can do it anywhere. This means that creating a mobile stitch studio is essential. You can easily carry it with you day to day without feeling like you're dragging your entire studio around. Here are my best tips for creating a mobile stitch studio:

—

Use a lightweight bag. You don't want to add extra weight to your daily purse or backpack—this is meant to help you through your day, not hinder it by making you feel like you're lugging around a boulder.

—

Use a lightweight pincushion substitute, such as a scrap piece of felt.

—

Take along a plastic sandwich bag for trash bits. Remember—snips of random thread are not a fashion statement.

—

Keep your thread, fabric, and main project in separate plastic bags. It's impressive how quickly everything can turn into a tangled mess when the elements of a project are allowed to mingle in one space, so it's best to keep them seperated.

—

Take only what you need for the project you're working on. I know this sounds obvious, but it's so easy to just keep adding items you might think you need. You'll overwhelm your project bag very quickly this way.

The Back of Your Work Does Not Matter

This is something I really want you to take away from our time together. While I admire stitchers who make the backs of their projects as neat as the fronts, it's simply not something that concerns me.

Hand stitching offers me special joy and peace. Fretting that every stitch I take on the front of my project could be causing a chaotic mess on the back sucks all the meditative qualities out of it. So let the backs of the work go free range and don't lose any sleep over it.

Tools and Tips for Stitching on Paper

Paper

Card stock

This is a medium- to heavy-weight paper that can be easily found in any craft store. Think scrapbooking paper—it has enough thickness to be stiff but not so much that you can't get a needle through it. It comes in pretty much every color and can be smooth or have texture.

Specialty paper

If you're fortunate enough to have a specialty paper store in your area, hide your credit card. It's impossible not to take several sheets home. These papers are made from the unusual, like cork, bark, or leaves. They can also have patterns formed directly into them or include materials trapped between layers. They are wonderful additions to any project featuring paper.

Mixed-media paper

This refers to paper that can handle a wide range of media, such as markers, watercolors, and paints (and, of course, hand stitching!). I usually buy pads of this paper in the craft store. Hot press paper has a smooth surface and cold press paper has a surface with texture.

Chipboard

This is a thick paper often made from recycled paper. It's most often used as the backing for items such as notepads. I love it for its plain appearance and strength.

A variety of papers (from top to bottom): specialty paper that has been molded to have a diamond pattern, colored rag paper, chipboard, medium-weight card stock, and a pad of mixed-media paper.

Tools

Screw punch

This tool is commonly used by book makers. It punches uniform holes into paper and, unlike a traditional hole punch, its reach is not limited. You can punch holes from ⅟₂₅" to ⅛" (1 to 4 mm). You need to use a cutting mat beneath, as it's a sharp tool and can damage surfaces.

Awl

An awl is like a giant needle attached to a handle. It's used for punching holes and comes in a variety of sizes.

Hole punch

This tool is used to punch circles in paper. It comes in different diameters and typically can only punch one size per tool. It has a handle similar to a pair of scissors, which makes its reach limited.

Cutting mat

This is a hard-surfaced mat, often with a grid showing measurement marks, that protects work surfaces from sharp tools, such as craft knives and rotary cutters.

Double-sided tape

This clear tape is sticky on both sides.

Masking tape

This paper-type tape is easy to tear and has a low-tack adhesive, making it easy to reposition if needed.

Craft knife

A craft knife, such as X-Acto, lets you get into small spaces and curves easily and precisely.

Selected tools for stitching on paper (from left to right): a screw punch, an awl, and a paper punch.

Paper Stitching Tips

Making a hole in paper is completely unforgiving. Once it's there, there's no going back. You can make holes with a screw punch, a hole punch, an awl, or an embroidery needle. If you're using an awl or an embroidery needle, punch the holes from the front of the project to the back because this does not remove material like a hole punch; it displaces it.

—

Avoid punching holes too closely together. The stability of paper greatly decreases when the holes are too close to each other, and you run the risk of tearing a hole in your project.

—

When starting or ending thread, it's easiest to secure these to the paper project using a piece of masking tape. This eliminates the bulk of knots and helps keep the project flat.

—

If you want to use layers of paper in a project, consider one of these two options to avoid making it too hard to stitch through:

Use thick paper on only one layer and very thin papers on the others.

If you want to use multiple layers of thicker paper, punch holes in each layer individually before combining for the project.

STITCHING
TECHNIQUES

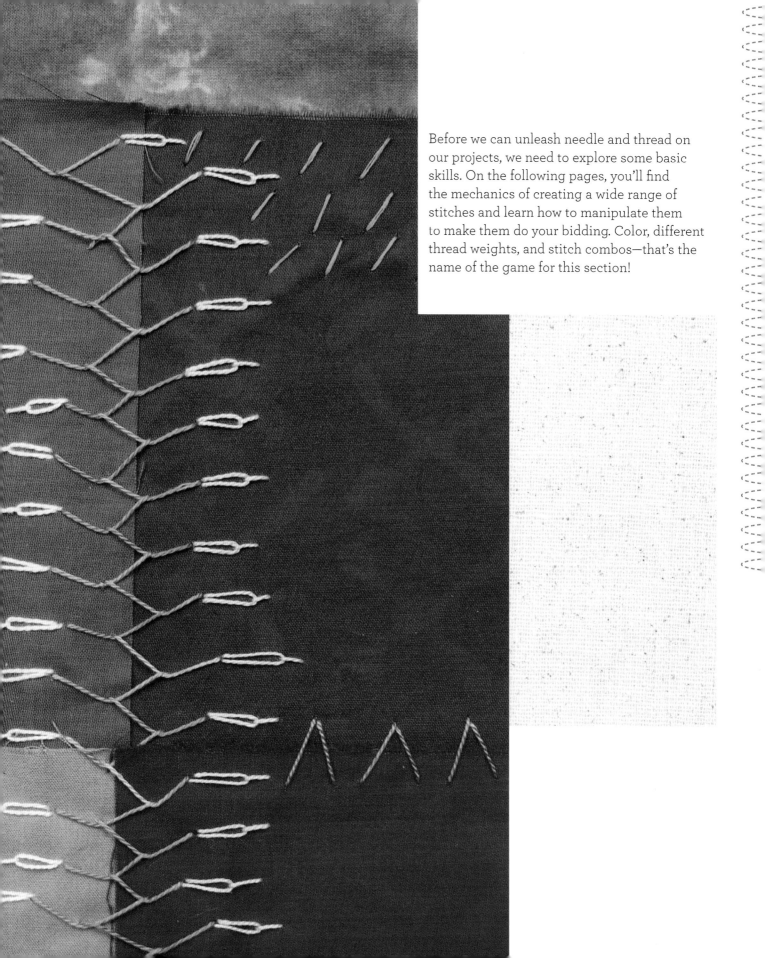

Before we can unleash needle and thread on our projects, we need to explore some basic skills. On the following pages, you'll find the mechanics of creating a wide range of stitches and learn how to manipulate them to make them do your bidding. Color, different thread weights, and stitch combos—that's the name of the game for this section!

Types of Stitches

The world of embroidery stitches is vast. But a stitch doesn't need to be a complicated contortionist trick to make an impact in a project. This section shows how to create a stitch step by step, as well as variations for increasing its interest level.

When I first learned to hand stitch, I created stitch squares. These squares are 4" × 4" (10.2 × 10.2 cm) pieces of felt on which I practiced not only how to create a specific stitch, but also how to manipulate it to look different. That's what we're going to do here.

Let's take a closer look at each stitch.

X Stitch

This is what I like to call a staple stitch. It's always there, waiting to be placed in a nook or cranny that just needs a little something. It's quite utilitarian but can have a wonderful effect when employed in various ways.

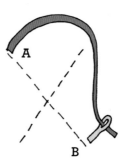 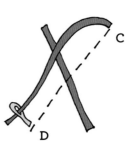 

Bring the thread up at A and down at B. Pull the thread through to lie flat against the fabric.

Bring the thread up at C and down at D. Pull the thread flat.

A completed X stitch.

Seed Stitch

Seed stitch creates a speckled surface that closely resembles shading.

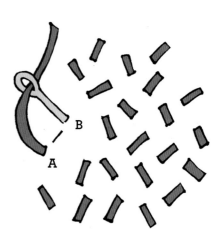

Bring the thread up at A and back down at B. Pull flat.

Repeat step 1 until you've covered the desired area.

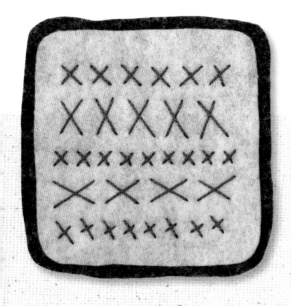

The square on the left shows examples of how the X stitch can be stretched and shrunk to create different looks.

The square on the right shows how effectively the X stitch can be used to create patterns, visual interest, and texture. Clockwise from top left: as a quick filler for large areas, stitching it in a varying sizes; making one of its legs much shorter; stacking them on top of one another to form a diamond pattern; and creating a giant X and filling it in with smaller ones.

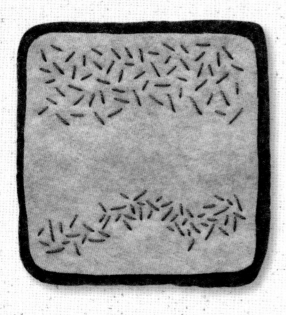

The square on the left shows an all-over pattern as well as one that has been "shaped" into a specific area.

The square on the right shows the effectiveness of seed stitch in defining spaces. Clockwise from top left: creating a shape by stitching dense seed stitches without an outline, creating the same shape by stitching negative space, adding seed stitches around an existing shape for texture, and creating an ombre effect with dense seed stitches at the bottom and looser ones at the top.

Backstitch

The backstitch creates a continuous line with no breaks between the stitches. It's like drawing with thread. It's awesome for creating images and adding texture.

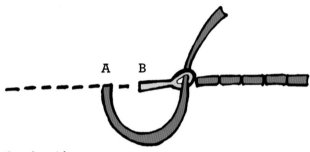

Bring the thread up at A. Bring the thread down at B and pull the thread flat against the fabric.

Arrow Stitch

The arrow stitch is essentially two straight stitches configured in an inverted V.

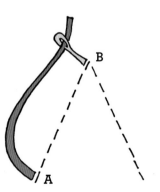 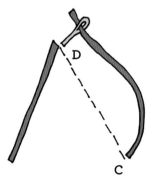 

Bring the thread up at A and then back down at B. Pull it flat against the fabric.

Bring the thread up at C and back down at D. Pull it flat.

A completed arrow stitch.

In the square on the left, the wrapped stitches (second from the top) were created by first completing a row of plain backstitch and then weaving a thread in and out of the stitches. The third and fourth rows, which look similar to the second row, were stitched differently. Instead of lining up the ends of the stitches, they were stacked slightly at an angle, and the two rows were stitched very closely together.

The square on the right shows the backstitch in different patterns.

The square on the left shows variations on the arrow stitch by stacking it and changing the length of its legs.

The square on the right shows how it can be used in a project. Clockwise from top left: filling a large arrow stitch with smaller ones, stacking them tightly to create a feather shape, connecting them to form diamond shapes, and overlapping them to create open filler stitches.

Running Stitch

Running stitch and backstitch (see pages 30–31) are very similar. The main difference is that running stitch leaves a gap between stitches. You can create interesting textural effects by altering the length of the gap. This stitch has been used for centuries and, in many cultures, it's the main stitch used in embroidery. There is beauty in its simplicity, and I encourage you not to disregard it because it's more basic than other stitches.

Bring the needle up at A and down at B in one motion.

Leave a small gap between the stitches. Go up at C and down at D in one motion.

Continue the line by doing the up and down of the stitch in single motions.

Satin Stitch

Satin stitch is the ultimate filler stitch. It can sometimes feel intimidating because it seems like you're going to be stitching forever. It's definitely more of a marathon than a sprint, but it creates such a beautiful surface that I continuously find myself going back to it.

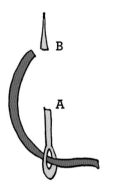

Bring the needle down at A and up at B in one motion.

Repeat step 1 until the area has been filled in.

I like to stitch satin stitch two different ways—dense (which is the traditional method) and loose. The dense version is accomplished by placing the stitches very close to one another so that you can't see under it. The loose version is done by leaving more space between the stitches.

I actually begin dense satin stitch with a loose version and then go back and fill in the gaps. This is easier for me to keep the shape I am trying to stitch and helps prevent the holes created by the needle from morphing into one giant tear, particularly on paper.

The square on the left shows easy variations of the stitch. The second row shows it broken up, creating almost an industrial-looking kind of stitch pattern.

The square on the right shows various ways running stitch can be used to create interesting filler effects. Stitching it in curves is easily accomplished by keeping the stitches shorter around the rounded areas.

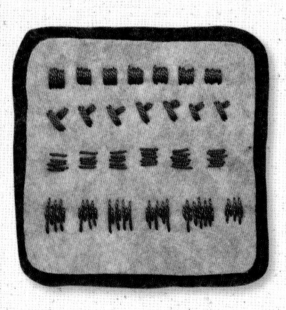

Both loose and dense versions are easily altered by varying their stitch length. The square on the left shows this. The top two rows are dense satin stitch and the bottom two rows are loose satin stitch.

The square on the right shows the stitch in action. The top two squares show the dense version, which is great for creating bold imagery or a frame in corners. The bottom two squares show the energy that loose satin stitch can have when stacked or lined up in varying heights.

Fly Stitch

The fly stitch has an organic feel to it and lends itself well to creating movement in a stitch pattern.

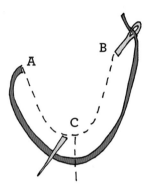

Bring the thread up at A and down at B, passing the thread underneath the needle at point C. Pull the thread flat but use light tension.

Take the thread down at point D and pull flat.

Lazy Daisy Stitch

The lazy daisy may be named after a flower, but that doesn't mean you have to use it for only that.

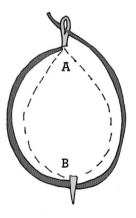

Bring the thread up at A and down at B, passing the thread underneath the needle at point B. Pull the thread flat but with very loose tension.

Take the thread down at point C and pull flat.

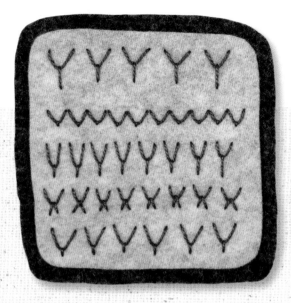

The square on the left shows the different ways to alter individual fly stitches.

The square on the right shows how to use fly stitch in a project. Clockwise from top left: in a circle to create a frame to fill in with other stitches; in altered lengths to create a soft zigzag movement, stacked to emulate retro patterns, and with long straight legs to create a segmented area in the center that can be filled in with smaller fly stitches.

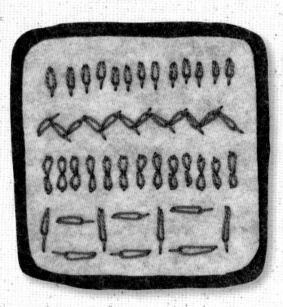

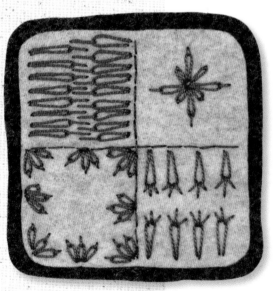

The square on the left shows that simply by tilting and stacking the lazy daisy stitch, you can achieve some very interesting effects.

The square on the right shows, clockwise, extra-long loops and straight portions stitched closely together to fill space, a circle with varying lengths to create shapes like stars and flowers, straight stitches to alter the feel of the stitch completely, and accents for a frame around a stitching motif.

Blanket Stitch

The blanket stitch is a utilitarian stitch that can be used to secure the edges of a project and has the potential to add some movement to your stitched artwork.

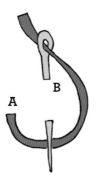  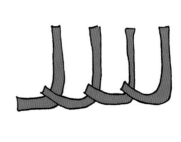

Bring the needle up at A and allow the thread to form a loose loop that goes underneath the needle. Bring the thread down at B and come out even with where you came up at A; this is done in one motion. Pull the thread flat.

Go down at C, again allowing the thread to loop beneath the needle and come back up through the fabric even with the bottom of the last stitch. Pull the thread flat.

Repeat for the desired length.

Chain Stitch

Chain stitch is a series of loops stitched in succession, with no break between them. It can be used to create the base for combination stitching or used alone in straight lines and curved shapes.

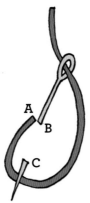  

Bring the thread up at A and allow the thread to form a loose loop. Bring the needle down at B and up at C in one motion, trapping the thread beneath the needle. Pull the thread flat.

Bring the needle up at D and allow the thread to form a loose loop. Bring the needle down close to D and up at E in one motion, trapping the thread beneath the needle. Pull the thread flat.

Repeat for the desired length.

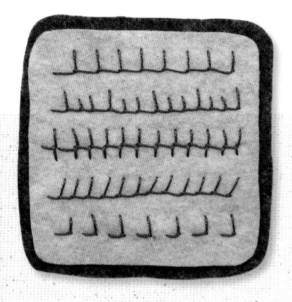

The square on the left shows blanket stitch variations that can be accomplished when stitched in rows. Altering the height of the vertical leg or slanting it can add interest.

The square on the right shows the stitch as a filler and a way to create circular motifs.

Add extra drama by creating very long stitches alongside very short stitches.

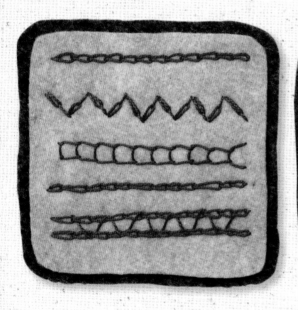

The square on the left shows variations on the chain stitch by adding more distance at the base of each new stitch and weaving threads between two rows of stitch.

The square on the right shows how to manipulate chain stitch into different shapes. Clockwise from top left: creating a filler stitch by zigzagging the chain stitch, creating curved shapes by alternating long chains with smaller chains, creating a dense circle with rows of chain stitch, and laying down a contrasting color of thread and stitching over the top to create a two-color effect.

French Knot

The French knot gets a bad rap for being a difficult stitch. Once you master it, though, you can use it in a variety of ways. Its strength comes from its ability to play nicely with other stitches.

 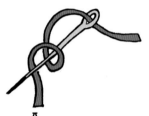 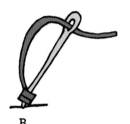

A

A

B

Bring the thread up at A and move the thread behind the needle.

Wrap the thread around the needle clockwise at least once. I like to do two wraps.

Anchor the tip of the needle where you came up at A (this is now B) and pull the thread tight until it slides down the needle. Pull the needle through the fabric and pull the thread slowly through to secure the knot.

Vary the size of the knot by the number of wraps.

Feather Stitch

The feather stitch has awesome movement. It's got lots of energy and fills a space quickly. It also acts as a great foundation stitch for combination or improv stitching (see page 46).

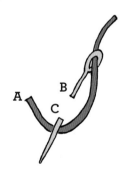 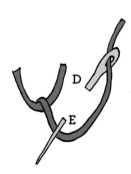 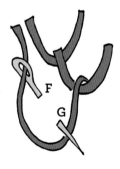 

Bring the thread up at A and allow the thread to form a loose loop. Bring the thread down at B and up at C in one motion, trapping the thread beneath the needle. Pull flat.

To the right of where you went down at C, go down at D and up at E in one motion, trapping the thread beneath the needle. Pull flat.

Repeat step 3, but this time start on the left side, bringing the thread down at F and up at G.

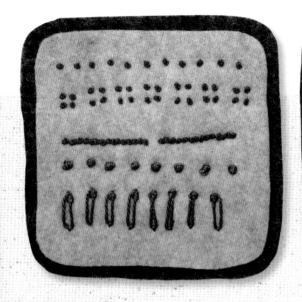

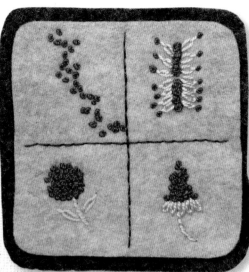

The square on the left shows the French knot as a pattern in groups; a tight line; and slightly distorted by leaving a long loop when pulling the thread back down.

The square on the right demonstrates how to use the French knot to stitch delicate imagery. Clockwise from top left: creating a spray of random filler stitching, combining French knots with lazy daisy stitches to create a frilly-looking seam treatment, stacking French knots in a triangle with added lazy daisy at the base and a backstitch stem to create a flower, and bunching French knots into a circle with a backstitch stem and lazy daisy leaves to create an abstract flower.

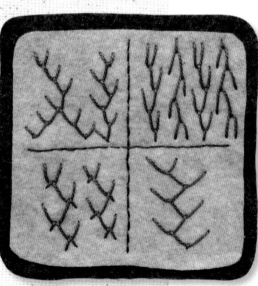

The square on the left shows how to manipulate the look of feather stitch by creating longer dips in the base of the stitch or more swoops before switching sides.

The square on the right shows fun variations. Clockwise from top left: multiple vertical rows of stitch next to each other create the illusion of continuous stitching, long dips create an organic stitch, extra wide and shallow dips create a dramatic cup-looking stitch, and adding a small straight stitch at the bottom of each dip creates a stitch that almost mimics the X stitch.

Thread Rose

The thread rose is a fun way to show off special and variegated threads.

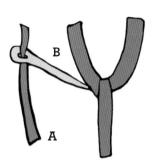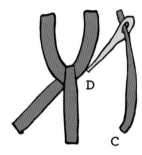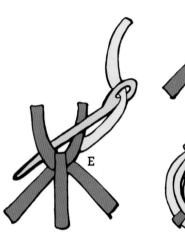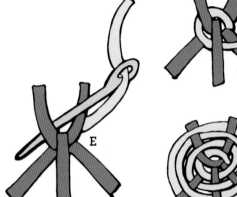

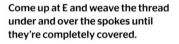

Stitch a fly stitch (see page 34). Come up at A and down at B.

Come up at C and down at D. After you come up at C, switch to a tapestry needle. These needles have blunt tips and won't snag your thread as you weave your rose.

Come up at E and weave the thread under and over the spokes until they're completely covered.

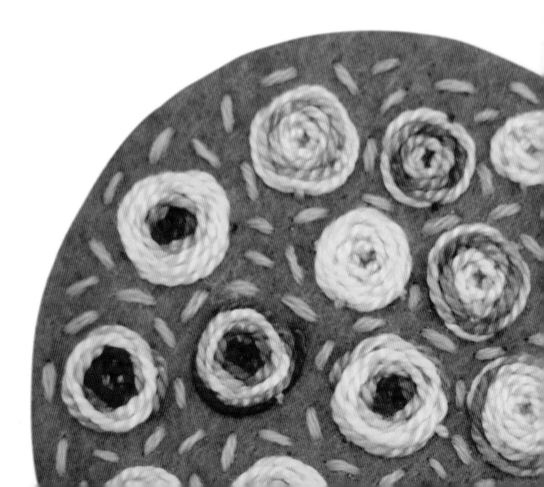

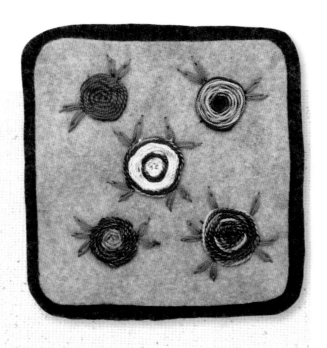

This square shows lazy daisy stitch leaves around the roses. It also demonstrates how different threads change the look of the rose. Clockwise from top left: solid orange thread; variegated thread with a long space between color shifts creating the illusion that several different threads were used; variegated thread with short spaces between color shifts; a pale center with a dark outer color; and alternating solid white thread with a variegated red thread.

Stitch Combinations

Every time I think about stitch combinations, I hear that song: "One is the loneliest number …" The stitches used here are nifty all on their own, and you can do a lot with them individually, but once you start stacking them together, then what? There's a kind of magic to that.

Here are examples of how to put them together for complicated-looking combinations. The order in which they were stitched is listed next to each stitch.

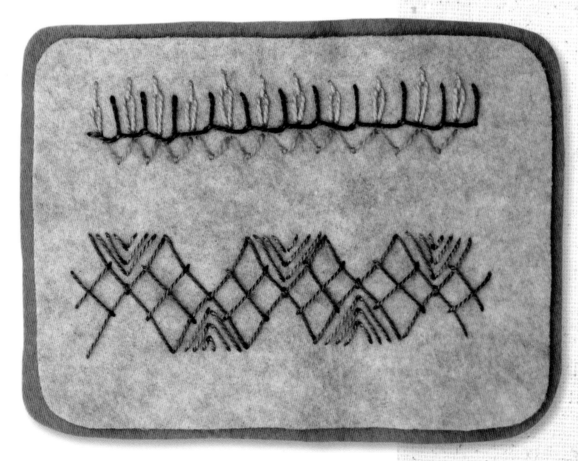

Top row stitch order:

1

Blanket stitch in brown thread.

2

Fly stitch with very short tack stitch in blue thread.

3

Lazy daisy in yellow thread.

– – – – – – – – – – – – – –

Bottom row stitch order:

1

Oversized X stitch in brown thread with tack stitch in the center to add stability.

2

Smaller X stitch in dark gray thread.

3

Stacked arrow stitches in pale purple thread.

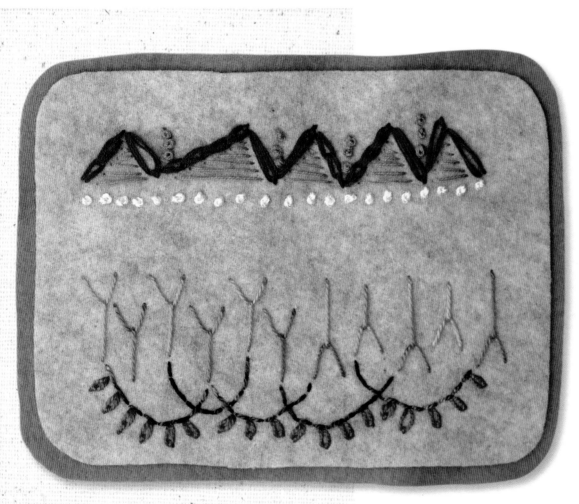

1

Chain stitch of uneven loops and spacing in red thread.

2

French knot in green thread.

3

Straight stitches in green thread.

4

French knots in white thread.

- - - - - - - - - - - -

Bottom row stitch order:

1

Fly stitch in variegated blue thread in various sizes and staggered spacing.

2

Backstitch in dark gray thread.

3

Short lazy daisy stitch in burnt orange thread.

Exploring Color

There are very few color combinations that I don't like. From vibrant, gaudy, and high-contrast hues to peaceful neutrals—love them all. Color sets the mood of your artwork, immediately letting the viewer know how you were feeling when you made it.

Harnessing color in your stitching allows you to build layers of interest in a way that other art forms can't. Because the stitches float on top of the surface you're working on, you can control the density and placement with as much or as little precision as you want.

I want to caution you, though, not to get so caught up in the academics of color that you forget the emotional impact it has on a piece.

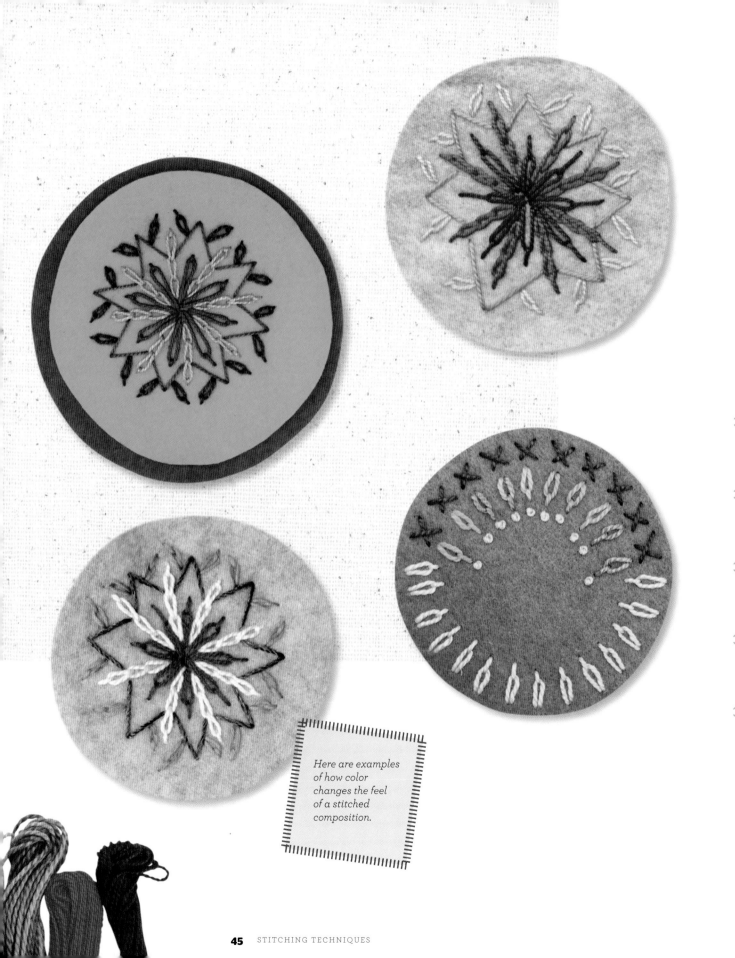

Here are examples of how color changes the feel of a stitched composition.

Improv Stitching

Improv stitching, or stitching on the fly, is incredibly fun and addictive. It's more of a gut reaction to your work than anything else, and the interpretation you apply to your work is entirely personal.

I can't tell you exact steps on how to do it, but I can offer you some tips and explain how *I* go about approaching it. Another element that makes improv exciting is mixing different thread weights together in the same composition. Incorporating thinner threads with thicker threads adds a sense of dimension.

Let's walk through a simple example of improv stitching.

1

Before you start improv stitching, take stock of the shapes you have to work with. Starting with stitches to fill in spaces at the edges helps create a framework for detail stitching later, if you want to add some.

In our example, I added varying sizes of X stitches on the inside and outside of the C shape, using the edges of it as the stopping point for those stitches.

The straight stitches on the C shape are there solely as a means to hold it down. I like to celebrate the structural stitches by giving them a prominent place.

Also notice the colors—the blue on the orange C gives a nod to the purple circle, and the reddish gold X stitches tie the purple and red circles together. It's like a conversation among the different layers.

3

The last step in our improv exercise is about adding little details. Now that the edges are filled in with some interesting stitching, we can start filling in the gaps.

I added three French knots at the ends of the fly stitches, each with a different number of wraps. I often use white as a punch of color because it offers some good contrast without being garish.

2

Continue to fill in the edges with stitching. I find it important to vary the types of stitches when doing improv stitching, as it creates a pleasant chaos that makes the piece more interesting.

But it's not all crazy stitching—there's some consideration to keep the stitching "conversation" going. I added long lazy daisy stitches in light blue along the remaining open edge. They mimic the rhythm of the X stitches on the other side without copying them exactly.

Also, the light blue thread is a heavier weight than the thread used for the X stitches. It adds some bulk to compete with the weight of the C on the other side.

In between the spaces of the long chain stitch, I tucked in some fly stitches in a size 12 thread. These stitches are much thinner than anything else used so far and they blend into the felt, creating a supporting design to build off of.

To be honest, I tend to stitch improv projects until they beg for mercy. I like the density and the challenge of squeezing in that one last stitch.

Give improv a chance. Build yourself some simple structure by stitching around the edges and then add lots of details. I promise you'll enjoy it!

Creating Your Own
Pattern for Stitching

There are a lot of wonderful patterns out there to stitch onto your work, but you can create one from something you love to make it more personal.

To help you understand how I create a pattern for stitching using a doodle based on a photo, I'm going to walk you through a design inspired by one of my favorite things: plants. I'm a complete nerd about them—I can't get enough of them.

Doodling Pattern Ideas

I'm one of those people who is more interested in details than in the overall view. I'll zero in on an interesting shape or color and become mesmerized. As an artist, this obsession with small elements is a constant source of inspiration that influences much of what I do.

That's where doodling comes in. My sketchbooks are full of what seem like random doodles, but the truth is that they all begin with a few specific elements adapted from something I find interesting. They often serve as an excellent base for creating designs that can be used for hand stitching. Carry your camera with you as you wander to capture things that strike your fancy.

When using a photo as visual inspiration, start by listing three things about it that pique your interest. Details that I love about the begonia, right, are:

—

The contrast between the colors in the leaves. The darker brown really makes the green look vibrant.

—

The irregular shapes of the leaves.

—

The way the veins of the leaves form thin interior boundaries, creating sections.

I'm a plant lover, and begonias are a personal favorite. They're serious show-offs in the detail department. I found this one particularly inspiring.

Using these three things as a jumping-off point, we can draw doodles of pattern ideas. How do you know when you're done? I recommend ending your doodle pattern when the space within the design is about half empty and half hatched. You want to leave breathing room to allow the stitching to evolve organically as you work. In other words, you don't have to figure out the entire design now.

Drawing the Pattern

1

Draw a simplified version of the leaf shape. Using one of the leaves as reference, draw in the veins to create sections.

2

Begin sectioning off parts of the drawing to designate areas for stitching. Add a border around the outside of the leaf and in two random sections of the vein pattern. Add hatch marks to these sections to keep track of the portions that will be cut out for the stencil.

3

Add random arcs. Begonias don't grow neatly—they swoop over on long stems in all different directions. The randomly placed curves help convey this energy. Add hatch marks to these sections as well.

This pattern can then be used to create a freezer-paper stencil. (See next page.)

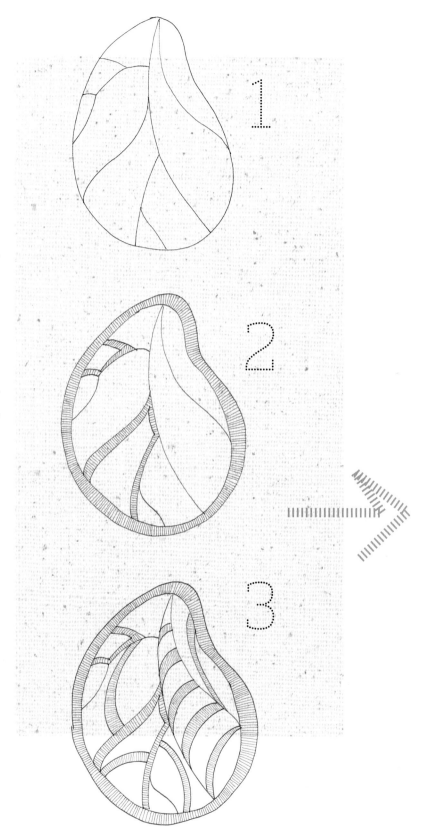

Making a Freezer-Paper Stencil

We've created this pattern for the Technicolor Begonia Cushion project (pages 88–91). So now we need to transfer the pattern onto the fabric. There are many ways that we can transfer a pattern, and for this particular project we're going to use a freezer-paper stencil. A freezer paper stencil is an easy way to capture delicate parts of a design and it's an inexpensive method for quick fabric printing.

M/A/T/E/R/I/A/L/S

Technicolor Begonia Cushion template (p. 131)

Masking tape

Cutting mat

Scissors

Freezer paper

Black marker

Craft knife

Iron and ironing board

14" × 14" (35.6 × 35.6 cm) piece of cotton fabric

Plastic sheet

1" (2.5 cm)-wide sponge brush

Fabric paint

1

Enlarge the Technicolor Begonia Cushion pattern to 115 percent.

2

Tape the copy of the pattern to the cutting mat at the four corners with masking tape.

3

Cut a piece of freezer paper that is about 1" to 2" (2.5 to 5 cm) bigger in each direction than the pattern and tape it paper side up over the leaf pattern (FIGURE A).

4

Using a marker, trace the design onto the freezer paper. Include the hatch marks as they will help you know where to cut (FIGURE B).

5

The hatched areas need to be cut out, but you need to leave a small bridge of freezer paper between sections so the stencil will hold together. Do this by cutting just inside each section with a craft knife.

Begin cutting the sections in the center because the stencil has the most stability when the outer edge is still part of the whole piece of freezer paper.

Once all the sections are cut out on the inside of the leaf, cut around the outer edge about 1" (2.5 cm) away from the outer border. Cut out the outer border around the leaf—this will create two pieces to the stencil (FIGURE C).

FIGURE [A]

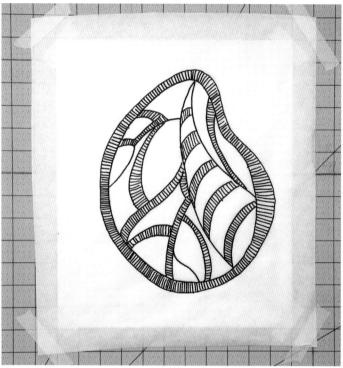

FIGURE [B]

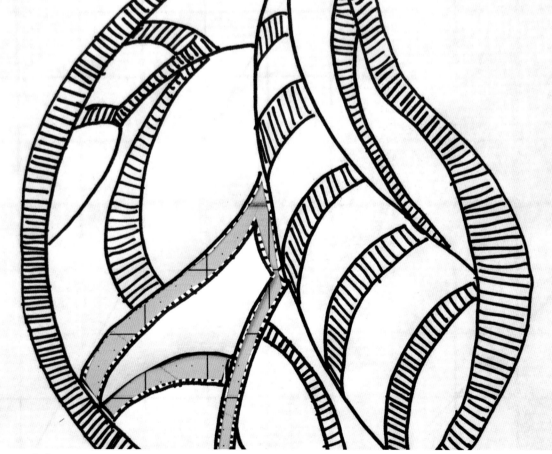

FIGURE [C]

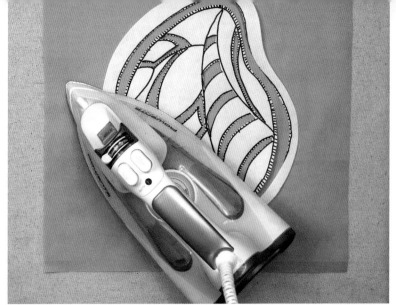

6

Remove the stencil from the cutting mat. Place your fabric onto an ironing board and position the stencil's shiny side against the cotton fabric.

7

Using an iron set to medium heat and no steam, iron the stencil onto the fabric. Do this by lifting the iron up and setting it down on the stencil—don't push the iron back and forth across the stencil or it will tear (FIGURE D).

FIGURE [D]

8

Place a plastic sheet over the work surface. Dip a sponge brush into fabric paint, dab the brush on the plastic sheet to remove any gobs of paint, and dab the stencil openings (FIGURE E).

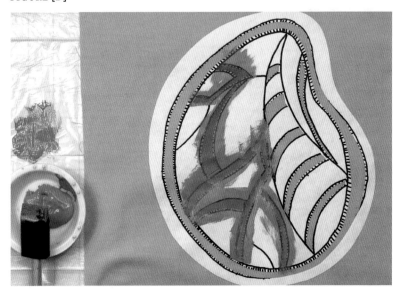

9

Don't wait for the paint to dry or the stencil could become stuck. Lift the stencil off slowly.

FIGURE [E]

10

Allow the paint to dry completely and then iron with a hot, dry iron to make the paint permanent (FIGURE F).

The pattern appears quite incomplete at this stage, and we did that on purpose. By keeping it fairly loose and using it as a guide, we have not forced ourselves to use specific stitching.

It's important when you create a pattern for stitching that you allow your creative muse some freedom to go with the flow. Nothing kills the joy of a creative project more than not being allowed to change your mind if you feel something else would work better!

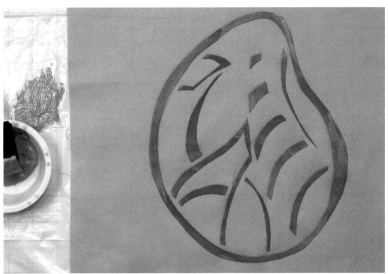

FIGURE [F]

Tips for Surface Design Projects

This book includes some fabric projects that feature surface design techniques, so here are a few things to keep in mind for your workspace:

—

When printing on fabric, create an easy and efficient printing surface. The bottom layer should be a piece of plastic, the middle layer a piece of felt, and the top layer a piece of canvas. The top layer will absorb any wet items like dye or paint and the plastic layer will protect your worktable from staining.

—

Always wash/clean your printing tools when you're done working with them so that they don't become damaged by dried paint or ink.

—

If you have sensitive skin, wear gloves when working with dye or paint.

—

Wear old clothes or an apron. Trust me, there's no such thing as "I can print this without getting anything on me." It can't happen, so be prepared to wear some of the things you're working with.

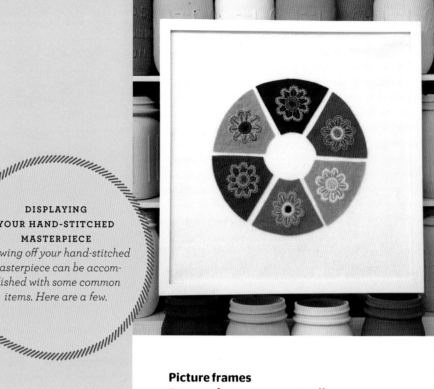

DISPLAYING YOUR HAND-STITCHED MASTERPIECE

Showing off your hand-stitched masterpiece can be accomplished with some common items. Here are a few.

Picture frames
Picture frames come in all sizes, shapes, and materials. Remove the glass from them, as this will only distort your artwork in the long run.

Old wood boxes or cigar boxes
Go vintage and upcycle discarded cigar or wood boxes to set your artwork in.

Cards
Blank cards offer an instant canvas for attaching work. They stand up on their own or can be hung to create an art installation.

Embroidery hoops
These are suitable for hand-stitched projects. They add a touch of whimsy and make it simple to show off your art.

Fabric and thread go together like peanut butter and jelly. It's a natural alliance and the different things that you can create with them are astounding. Fabric lends its fluidity to the stitching so they work together in harmony. From wearables to home décor to "I'm making this because it's FUN!," the fabric projects in this section cover all the bases.

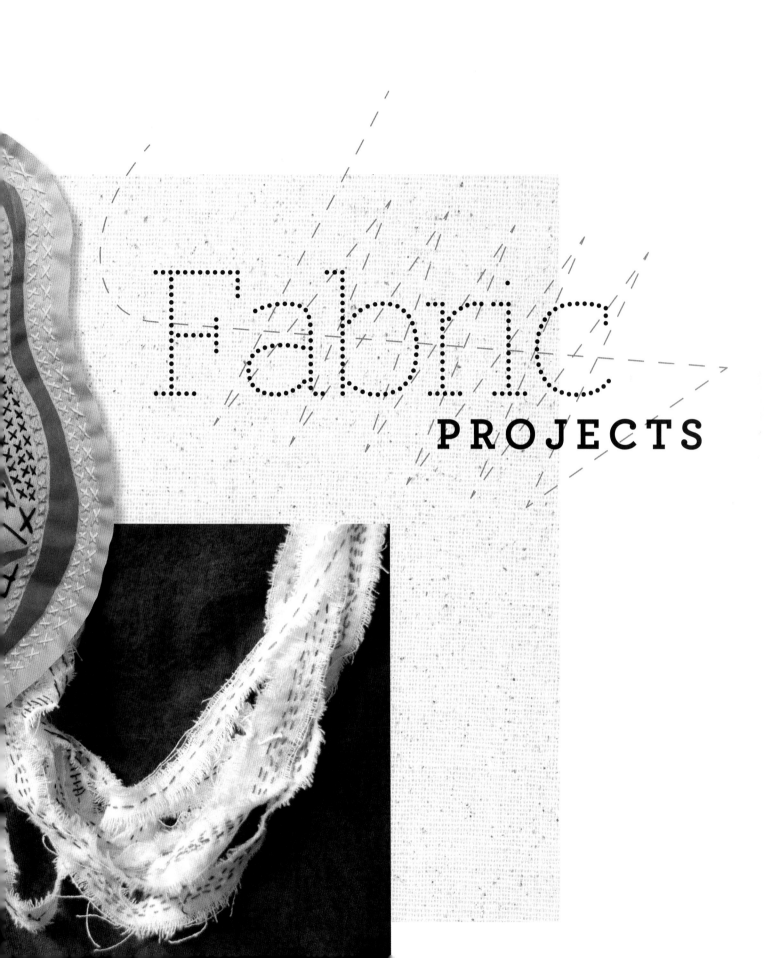

Fabric
PROJECTS

Stitched Buttons

Life is about the details, and this project honors that belief. Buttons are such small objects, but that doesn't mean they can't pack a punch. They have a wide range of uses, from clothing to mixed-media jewelry to closures on bags. Adding some hand stitching can personalize them and bring that final punch of special to your project. You can find cover button kits at craft stores.

M/A/T/E/R/I/A/L/S

Cover button kit with shanks on back and template to trace on fabric (size 45 or $1^1/_8$" [2.8 cm] button)

3"× 3" (7.6 × 7.6 cm) pieces of quilting-weight cotton in various solid colors

Fabric marking pen

Size 5 embroidery needle

2 strands of embroidery floss in five different colors

—

Note: Perle cotton is too bulky for this project because it will form lumps beneath the fabric.

Embroidery hoop (optional)

—

Note: If you want the extra support of a hoop to control your tension, you'll need larger pieces of fabric to fit inside of it. Do not double the fabric, or it will become too thick to assemble.

1

Trace the button template from the kit onto the fabric with a fabric marking pen (FIGURE A). (Note: The photo shows the template marked in dark black pen. This is for illustration purposes only. Use a marking pen that can be removed easily.)

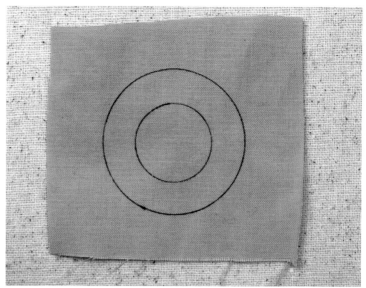

2

Use the embroidery needle and purple thread to blanket stitch (see page 36) around the line for the smaller circle. Keep the straight posts perpendicular to the circle. Stitch only to the edge of the smaller circle in the center. Stitching to the outer boundary will make the button difficult or impossible to assemble (FIGURE B).

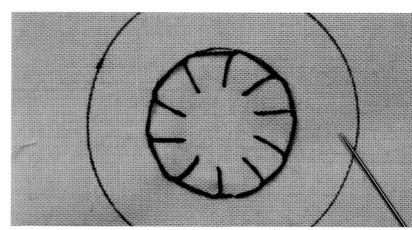

FIGURE [B]

3

Add a second row of blanket stitch so that it's nested inside of the first one. Bring the thread up below a straight bar of the first row of blanket stitch and go down between the gap created by the first row. Bring the thread back up below the next straight bar from the first row. Continue all the way around. This will create a slightly curved blanket stitch. Do not tie a stop knot in the thread. Leave a tail. This will get trapped between the two button halves when you assemble it (FIGURE C).

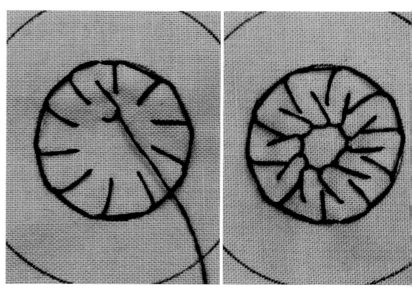

FIGURE [C]

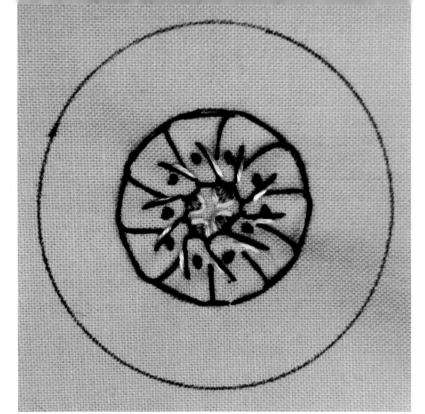

FIGURE [D]

4

Using yellow thread, stitch four fat lazy daisies (see page 34) in the center of the smallest circle. Make them fat by leaving a small distance between where you bring the thread up and where you take it back down at the base.

5

Using medium blue thread, satin stitch (see page 32) inside the yellow lazy daisies to fill them in. Using medium red thread, add French knots (see page 38) between the slanted bars of the second row of blanket stitch and in the very center of the button.

6

Using white thread, add a running stitch (see page 32) to one side of the slanted bars on the second row of blanket stitch. The stitching is complete at this point (FIGURE D).

7

Trim away the excess fabric at the big circle's outline. Trim the threads so that they do not extend past the edge of the fabric. This is what it should look like on the back (FIGURE E).

8

Assemble according to the button kit directions (FIGURE F).

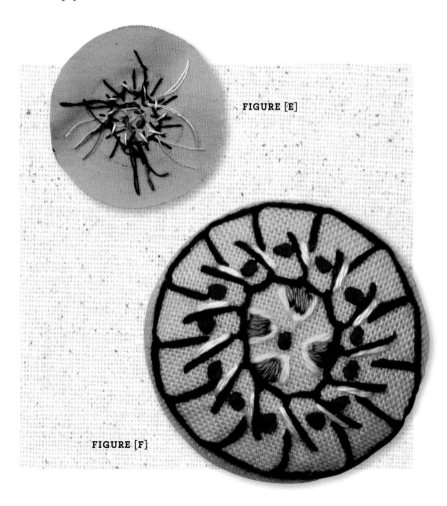

FIGURE [E]

FIGURE [F]

Strip-Stitched Fabric Necklace

Fabric and thread go with fashion like toast and butter. Often accessories like jewelry are made from stiff materials like metal or wood. But why should those substrates have all the fun? There's absolutely no reason why fabric can't also be jewelry.

This particular necklace lets fabric be itself. The frayed edges add to the texture. Using different weights of threads and colors also adds to a depth of interest. Only straight stitch is used on this project, showing its ability to stand strong as the primary design stitch. The delicate nature of the fabric demands an easy touch, a slow progression of layered stitching. I love this project because it's a kind of meditation and practice of patience.

M/A/T/E/R/I/A/L/S

9" × 24" (22.9 × 61 cm) piece of loose-weave fabric (I used raw silk.)

Thread in various weights, from perle 5 to sewing weight, and in variegated colors

Size 22 chenille needle

Size 5 embroidery needle

9" × 2½" (22.9 × 6.3 cm) piece of fabric

1

Tear the loose-weave fabric into seven ½" × 24" (1.3 × 61 cm) strips.

2

Using different weights and colors of threads, and the chenille and embroidery needles, add a running stitch (see page 32) to each strip (FIGURE A).

Be creative and add running stitches on the diagonal or arrow stitches (see page 30). Allow the knots in the start of the thread and the tails at the end of the stitching to show. They will add extra texture.

3

Once you have stitched all the strips, line up the ends and arrange them as you like. Take a couple of tack stitches at each end to secure the strips together as well as in two other locations to help them keep their shape (FIGURE B).

4

Lay about 1½" (3.8 cm) of the 9" × 2½" (22.9 × 6.3 cm) piece of fabric over one edge (FIGURE C).

Fold the fabric over and stitch it closed (FIGURE D). Repeat on the other side.

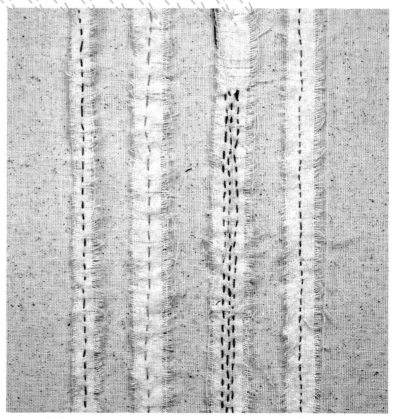

FIGURE [A]

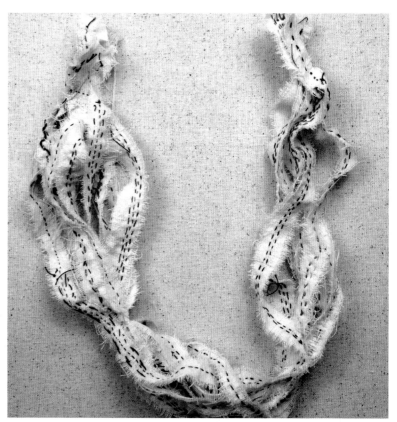

FIGURE [B]

FIGURE [C]

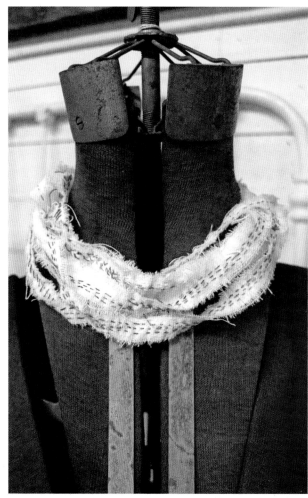

FIGURE [D]

DESIGN TIP
You can certainly tear more strips if you want a fuller necklace. You can also adjust the widths of the strips for variation.

Boho Collage Coasters

Every day for me begins with an enormous cup of coffee. I'm so not a morning person, and this magical drink snaps me out of the grumps and into a pleasant human being. My love for coffee has led to a strong affection for coffee cups and things to set them on. Something so awesome should have a pretty perch, don't you agree?

My studio is in no short supply of fabric scraps, so this project gathers them and uses improv stitching (see page 46) to create a special place to park your morning cup of coffee.

M/A/T/E/R/I/A/L/S

Boho Collage Coaster templates (pp. 127–128)

Scissors

Fabric marking pen

6 to 8 pieces of fabric of various weights and fiber content (for example, felt, home décor fabrics, silk, gauze, or cheesecloth)

Sewing machine-weight thread or pins (for basting)

Floss or thin thread (I used two strands of size 16 perle cotton.)

Size 5 embroidery needle

1

Scan and print the templates per the instructions on page 126. Cut out the templates with scissors. Use the fabric marking pen to trace the templates onto the wrong side of each fabric in the following quantities:

Two each of templates 1, 2, and 5

One each of templates 3 and 4

2

For the circles traced from template 1: Cut one exactly the size of the template and cut the second circle about ¼" outside the traced line so it will be a little bigger than the template (FIGURE A).

For template 2, cut one circle exactly the size of the template and one circle just inside the traced line so it's a little smaller than the template (FIGURE B). I used dyed cheesecloth for my smaller circle to add textural interest.

For templates 3 and 4, cut your fabrics on the traced line (FIGURE C).

For template 5, cut one circle exactly the size of the template and one circle just inside the traced line so it's a little smaller than the template (FIGURE D).

3

Stack the fabrics from largest to smallest, adjusting the arrangement until you're happy with it. Push them off-center to create visual interest (FIGURE E). Baste-stitch the layers together or pin them to hold them in place while you work.

4

Using the tips and tricks from the improv stitching exercises (see page 46), work from the center of the coaster outward to create your stitching composition. Remember to add stitching first to the outer edges of each shape and then go back and fill in (FIGURE F).

DESIGN TIP
Don't feel obligated to cut out solid circles. Play with different variations to create visual interest.

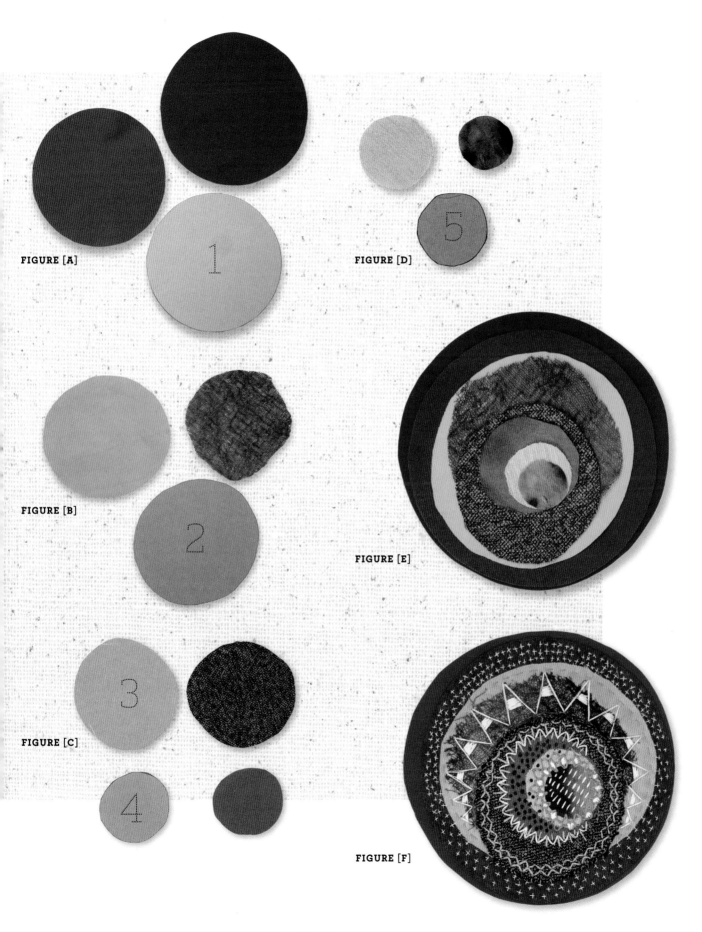

FIGURE [A]

FIGURE [B]

FIGURE [C]

FIGURE [D]

FIGURE [E]

FIGURE [F]

1

2

3

4

5

Coffee-Addict Kitchen Towel

Whether we realize it or not, our days contain rituals. Small ones, such as drinking our morning coffee, is an integral part of how we choose to begin each day.

It's no secret that I am a coffee addict. I say that I can't exist without it, and while it's true that the caffeine is much appreciated, it's the way I signal that my day is ready to begin. It forces a pause in the morning when the instinct is to hurry and frantically go about the daily tasks.

This kitchen towel is a "company" towel—you know the kind. The one that hangs in the kitchen to be admired. It's made even more special by some dye treatments to both the towel and one of the threads used. The inspiration for the poppies stitched between the steam swirls comes from my love of Meakin coffee pots, beautifully decorated ceramic pots bearing a wide range of designs, my favorite of which is the poppy pot.

This little towel bears so much of what I love about textiles—pattern creation, dyeing, stitching, and adding personal imagery. It's a grand way to recognize a daily ritual that many of us enjoy.

M/A/T/E/R/I/A/L/S

Jacquard indigo dye kit

28" × 17" (71 × 43 cm) natural color linen towel

Brewed coffee

1 skein white, size 5 perle cotton embroidery thread

Scissors

Embroidery transfer paper

Coffee-Addict Kitchen Towel template (p. 129)

Dull-pointed stylus

Embroidery thread in the following sizes and colors:
white, size 8 cotton perle
brown, size 5 cotton perle
black, size 5 cotton perle
red, size 5 cotton perle

Size 20 chenille needle

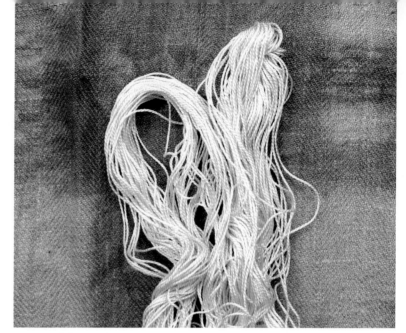

FIGURE [A]

1

Using indigo dye might sound mysterious and impossible to accomplish, but a dye kit makes it a snap. You'll have all the ingredients you need to dye the pattern shown on the towel. Follow the directions on the package. The kit makes a 4-gallon (4 L) vat of dye. Have a dye day with friends and experiment with all the different ways to apply this dye to textiles!

2

Add a special touch to the thread used on the towel by coffee dyeing white size 5 perle cotton thread. Brew some strong coffee and soak the thread in it overnight. This is not a true dye—it's more of a stain— and although the color will be pale, it will have a lovely ecru shade (FIGURE A).

3

Fold the towel into thirds lengthwise. The stitched pattern will be centered on the middle fold.

4

Scan and print the templates per the instructions on page 126. With scissors, cut a piece of transfer paper to the size of the stitch pattern on the template. Place the transfer paper beneath the stitch pattern, lining it up with the edge of the towel. Using a blunt stylus, trace over the pattern. Apply firm pressure so that the pattern will transfer to the fabric (FIGURE B).

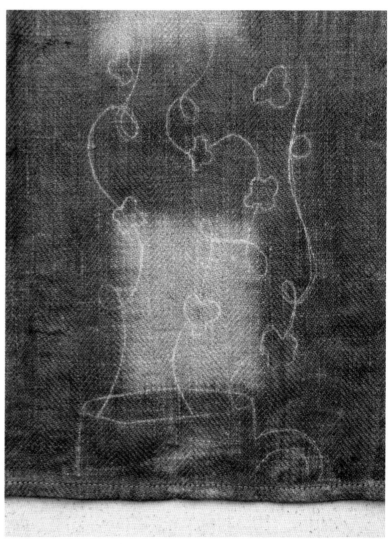

FIGURE [B]

5

Using the coffee-dyed thread and chenille needle, outline the coffee cup using backstitch (see page 30). Using the size 8 white perle cotton and a chain stitch with varying size loops (see page 36), stitch the swirls up to the points where the poppies will be stitched (FIGURE C).

6

Fill in the remainder of the coffee cup using backstitch. Stitch the coffee with brown thread and overlapping seed stitch (see page 28). Create the poppies by first stitching the centers with black thread and seed stitch. Then add satin stitch (see page 32) in red thread from the edge of the centers to the edge of the transferred shape (FIGURE D).

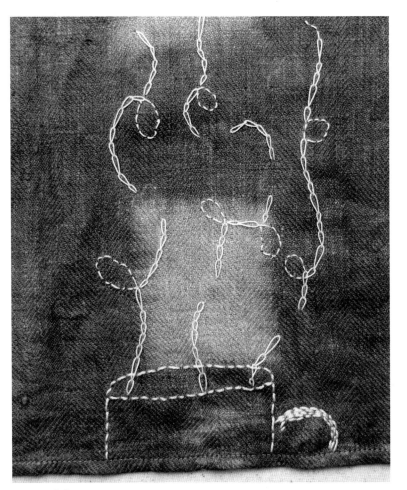

FIGURE [C]

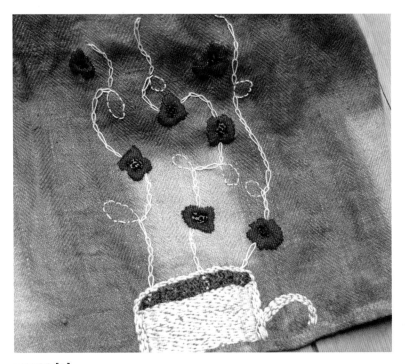

FIGURE [D]

Deconstructed Needle Book

Hand stitching can be a lot like babysitting a two-year-old—take your eye off your needle for three seconds and it goes missing, moving on to cause nothing but mischief.

If there is one thing that I've learned after twenty years of stitching it's this: you *must* have a place to safely keep your needles and pins. I've had many needle books over the years, but there has always been something I wished was different about every one. So I decided to design my own.

This needle book is not bound; all of the pages are a generous size and can be separated to only the ones you need for a particular project. Tuck the remaining ones safely away as you work. The book also has plenty of blank spaces, allowing you to record special projects by adding a stitch to the pages here and there. This needle book is a great project to show off variegated thread.

M/A/T/E/R/I/A/L/S

Craft knife

Cutting mat

Two 6" × 6" (15.2 × 15.2 cm) pieces of book board, 0.087" (2 mm) thick

Rotary cutter

1 yard (91 cm) white linen fabric

Six 6" × 6" (15.2 × 15.2 cm) pieces of felt in a variety of colors

One 5" × 14" (12.7 × 35.6 cm) piece of felt

One 4" × 4" (10.2 × 10.2 cm) piece of felt

One 1½" × 50" (3.8 × 127 cm) piece of fabric (to use as the tie for the book)

Size 5 embroidery thread in various colors (to add accents to the pages)

Size 18 chenille needle

Pins

Glue stick

Craft glue

1

Using a craft knife on a cutting mat, cut the book board into two 6" × 6" (12.7 × 12.7 cm) squares. If you do not have access to book board, you can upcycle cardboard boxes for this step.

2

With a rotary cutter and the cutting mat, cut the linen to the following sizes:

Four 6" × 12" (12.7 × 25.4 cm) rectangles

Two 6" × 17" (12.7 × 43.2 cm) rectangles

Three 6" × 14" (12.7 × 35.6 cm) rectangles

3

Take a 6" × 12" (12.7 × 25.4 cm) piece of linen and fold it over a 6" × 6" (15.2 × 15.2 cm) piece of felt so that it covers the entire square (FIGURE A).

4

Using light gray size 5 perle cotton and the chenille needle, blanket stitch (see page 36) the two open edges along the sides, leaving the edge opposite the folding edge open to allow the felt color to show through (FIGURE B).

5

Repeat steps 3 and 4 for a total of four pages. Add stitched details to the pages to add interest (FIGURE C).

FIGURE [A]

FIGURE [B]

FIGURE [C]

DESIGN TIP
I like raw edges on fabric. If you prefer a more finished edge, cut your fabric large enough to turn the edges under. Remember to add ¼" (6.4 mm) to each edge.

6

Wrap a 6" × 17" (12.7 × 43.2 cm) piece of linen around a 6" × 6" (15.2 × 15.2 cm) piece of felt. Fold the extra fabric back on itself to create a pocket to put items in. Tuck the raw edge under to create a finished look (FIGURE D).

7

Once you've created the size pocket you want, pin it in place. Using a combination of stitches, stitch along the top edge of the pocket to create the finished edge. Stitch only through the linen, not through the felt. Blanket stitch the two sides of the page as described in step 4 (FIGURE E).

8

Repeat steps 6 and 7 to make a total of two pocket pages.

9

Take one of the book board pieces and wrap a 6" × 14" (12.7 × 35.6 cm) piece of linen around it, securing it to the board with a glue stick (FIGURE F).

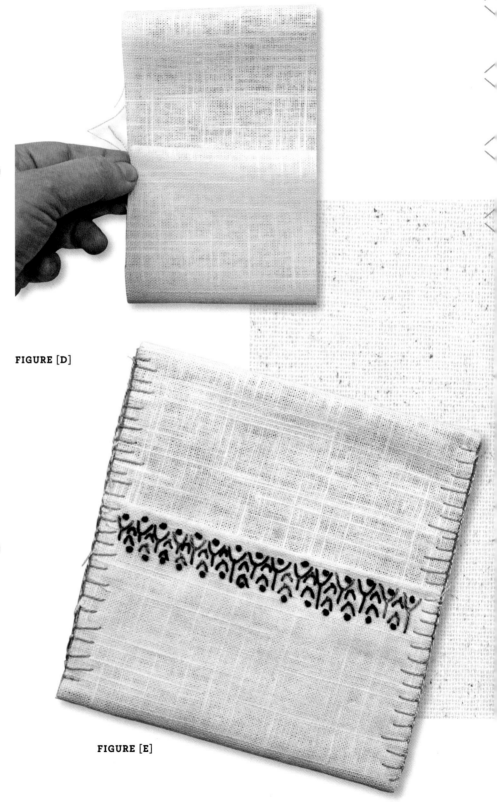

FIGURE [D]

FIGURE [E]

10

Wrap the 5" × 14" (12.7 × 35.6 cm) piece of felt around the linen in the other direction to cover the exposed edges, securing it to the covered board and itself with craft glue. This completes the back cover of the needle book.

11

On the 4" × 4" (10.2 × 10.2 cm) felt square, stitch a design to act as the cover for your needle book (FIGURE G).

12

For the front board, wrap the remaining two pieces of 6" × 14" (12.7 × 35.6 cm) linen around the board in both directions to cover the exposed edges. Adhere the stitched 4" × 4" (10.2 × 10.2 cm) piece of felt to the linen using craft glue.

13

Using the 1½" × 50" (3.8 × 127 cm) strip of fabric, tie your needle book together (FIGURE H).

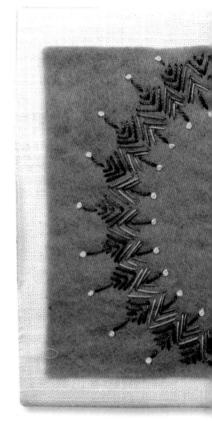

FIGURE [G]

FIGURE [F]

FIGURE [H]

Color-Wedge Stitched Sampler

Color has an enormous amount of control over our artwork. It conveys mood, energy, and emotion. When we think of the color wheel, we immediately picture a vibrantly colored circle split into six sections bearing pure red, yellow, orange, green, blue, and purple. There are so many variations of each color that it would be impossible to record them all. The world beyond the primary color wheel is vast, and in this project, we pay homage to all the different tones of each color.

The flower stitched on each wedge is influenced by my love of Polish folk embroidery, which is part of my heritage, and it's always a celebration of color and incredible skill. This color wheel gives you the opportunity to embrace the tones and shifts in each color family. Look around your environment at the colors that keep you company in your daily life. Stitch those into your color wheel, and record them in felt and thread.

M/A/T/E/R/I/A/L/S

Scissors or rotary cutter

Cutting mat

Water-soluble stabilizer

Color-Wedge Stitched Sampler templates (p. 130)

Marking pen

Six 4" × 4" (10.2 × 10.2 cm) pieces of felt, one each in red, orange, yellow, blue, green, and purple. You don't need to choose primary colors; you can choose shades.

Pins

White embroidery floss

Size 5 embroidery needle

4 different shades of embroidery thread in each color of the color wheel

A picture frame that can accommodate 12" × 12" (30.5 × 30.5 cm) artwork

One 12" x 12" (30.5 × 30.5 cm) piece of white felt

One 12" × 12" (30.5 × 30.5 cm) piece of white card stock

Double-sided tape

Craft glue

1

With scissors or a rotary cutter and cutting mat, cut six 4" × 4" (10.2 × 10.2 cm) pieces of water-soluble stabilizer. This is larger than what you will need to transfer the Color Wedge Folk Art Flower to each wedge, but it is easier to work with water-soluble stabilizer if the piece is bigger.

2

Download the templates per the instructions on page 126. With a marking pen, trace the Color Wedge Folk Art Flower onto each piece of water-soluble stabilizer.

3

Trace the Color Wedge template onto each piece of felt. Cut out the shapes.

4

Center the traced flower onto each wedge and pin in place.

5

Using two strands of white embroidery floss and the embroidery needle, back-stitch (see page 30) over the flower. You'll stitch through the felt and the stabilizer with each stitch. Do this for the entire outline on each wedge (FIGURE A).

6

Once you have completed the outline on a wedge, fill a small container with hot tap water and soak the felt piece for a few minutes. Rinse with cool water to remove the remaining stabilizer. Set aside to dry completely (FIGURE B).

FIGURE [A]

TECHNIQUE TIP

If you're using wool felt, do not agitate the material too much when removing the stabilizer. It can cause it to fuzz. You may want to soak each wedge in its own bath to avoid any possible color bleed.

FIGURE [B]

7

Fill in the center ring and the outer ring of each petal with dense satin stitch (see page 32), using a different shade thread of the color wedge for each one (FIGURE C).

8

Stitch French knots (see page 38) in a shade of the color wedge in the center circle. Add a single long running stitch (see page 32) to the center of each petal using the final shade of thread for the color wedge you chose (FIGURE D).

9

Remove the glass from the picture frame and set it aside. (We will not be using it in this project.) Secure the white felt to the white card stock using double-sided tape. Place it in the frame and replace the frame backing.

10

Position the color wedges 2" (5 cm) in from the frame on all sides and secure with a small amount of glue. (Avoid using too much glue; you don't want it to bleed through the felt. You can always add more later if needed.)

FIGURE [C]

FIGURE [D]

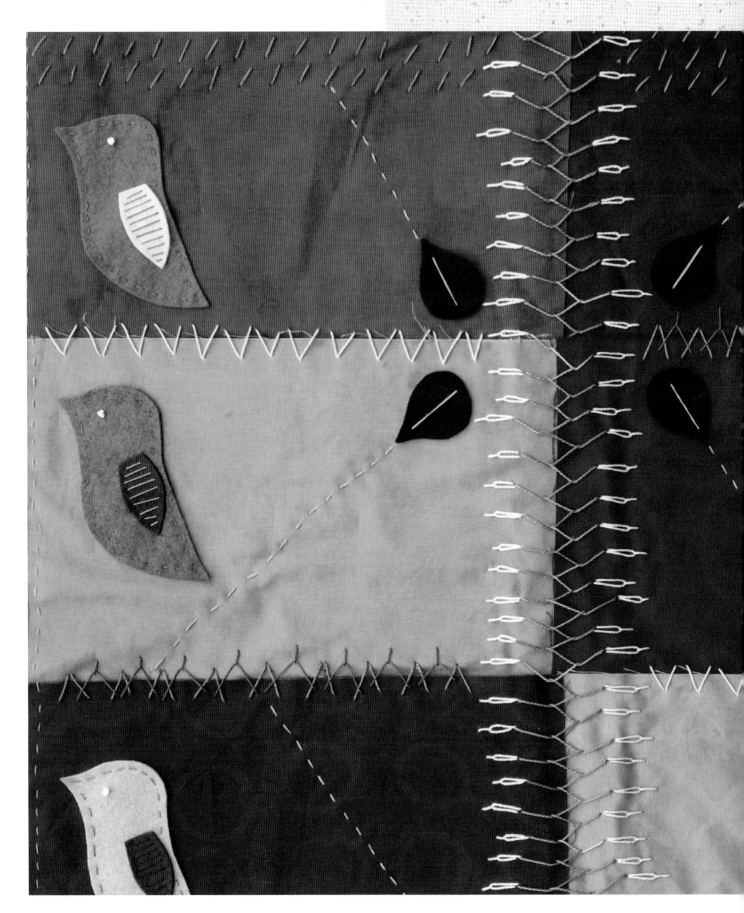

Doodle Love Lap Quilt

The word *quilt* is used loosely for this project. It bears a strong resemblance, but it's missing two quilting components commonly used—batting and binding.

I started my fiber-art obsession with crazy quilts and they continue to shape much of my current work. Crazy quilts are usually just two layers of fabric and are primarily a place to display embroidery and embellishment. (Which is one of the reasons I love them so.) I like to leave the edges raw, letting them have some personality by showing their wear over time.

The truth is that I use my laptop a lot—to write, draw, and edit photos. It's rarely far from my side. I often find myself wishing I had a light-weight, fun little quilt to drape across my legs. Something quirky to ground me in the nontechnical world. This little quilt is just that—little. It's not meant to cover your entire body, and it's got several elements that lend themselves to tactile fascination.

M/A/T/E/R/I/A/L/S

Plastic trash bags

Five 18" × 22" (45.6 × 55.9 cm) (fat quarter) pieces of 100% quilting cotton in various colors (This is more than you need, but when printing fabric, it's always better to have more than less, so you can choose the portions you like best.)

Washable school gel glue

Liquid Rit dye in Pearl Grey and Lemon Yellow

Plastic container

1 teaspoon measuring spoon

1 cup (235 ml) measuring cup

Rubber gloves

Iron

Rotary cutter

Cutting mat

1 yard (91 cm) hand-dyed fabric for quilt back

Pins

Size 5 perle cotton in a variety of colors

Size 20 chenille needle

Doodle Love Raindrop and Doodle Love Bird templates (p. 130)

Scissors

Fabric marking pen

Felt scraps in a variety of colors

Creating the Glue Gel Resist and Dyeing the Fabric

We start this project by printing an X and O pattern on the fat quarters to create custom-printed fabric. I strongly recommend 100 percent cotton, and the school *gel* glue, which is the easiest to remove. White school glue cannot be removed.

Glue gel resist is a faux batik process. The dried glue creates a resist on the fabric, meaning it will preserve the original color of the fabric by blocking out any dye placed over it. What makes this a faux process is that the glue breaks down very easily so when we dye our fabric, we have to use much lower heat and can't allow the fabric to sit for a deep shade of dye color. This gives us a subtle wash effect rather than a drastic color difference.

1

Prepare your work surface by laying down a piece of plastic. (A plastic trash bag cut open works fine.)

2

Lay your fabric down on the plastic and add an X and O pattern with the gel glue across the entire piece (FIGURE A). Repeat for all the fabrics.

3

Do not hang the fabric to dry because this will cause the glue to run. Move the plastic that the fabric is lying on to a place where the fabric can dry. Let the glue dry completely—it will seep through the fabric to act as a resist, and this can only be accomplished by giving it ample time to dry. I like to make the resist for this kind of fabric before I go to bed, and then it has the night to dry.

4

Once the glue is completely dry, prepare your dye wash in a plastic bucket with 2 teaspoons dye to 5 cups (1200 ml) warm tap water. Do not use boiling water or it will break the glue down too quickly. Use the hottest tap water you have. I used Lemon Yellow liquid Rit on the two paler colors of fabric and Pearl Grey liquid Rit on the three other darker colors.

5

Put on rubber gloves. Lay the fabric with the gel resist into the dye bath; don't agitate. Allow the fabric to soak for 10 minutes. Do not leave it for longer or the glue may break down and the dye will seep into the blocked areas. Rinse the fabric in hot tap water, gently rubbing it together to loosen up the glue. Hang to dry. You won't remove all the glue in this step.

6

Place the fabric back in the plastic container and pour very hot water over it. Let it soak until the water is cool. Rinse under tap water and hang to dry. It may take another soak and rinse to get all the glue out, but it's better to remove it in stages than to stress the fabric by removing it all at once.

7

After all the glue has been removed, iron the fabric. Using a rotary cutter and cutting mat, cut it into 12" × 7" (30.5 × 17.8 cm) pieces for a total of eight rectangles (FIGURE B).

TIP
Be generous with the glue. You want to see it sitting up from the surface, as shown in the photo.

FIGURE [A]

FIGURE [B]

Creating the Quilt

1

Lay out the backing fabric right side down. Arrange the rectangles on top of the backing fabric, right side up, in a color order that you find pleasing. Pin in place (FIGURE C).

2

With perle cotton and a chenille needle, stitch a wide feather stitch (see page 38) down the center of the quilt (FIGURE D).

3

Place lazy daisies (see page 34) at the edges of the wide feather stitch. Add a slanted long running stitch (see page 32) along the top and arrow stitch (see page 30) along the horizontal seams (FIGURE E).

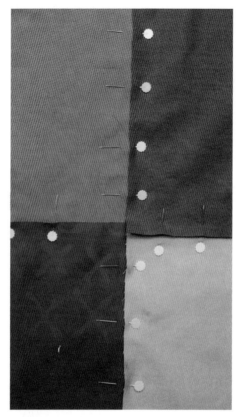

FIGURE [C]

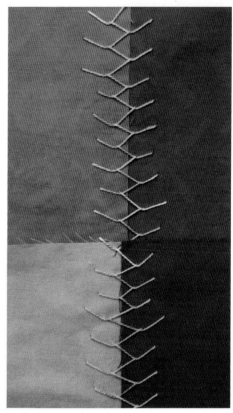

FIGURE [D]

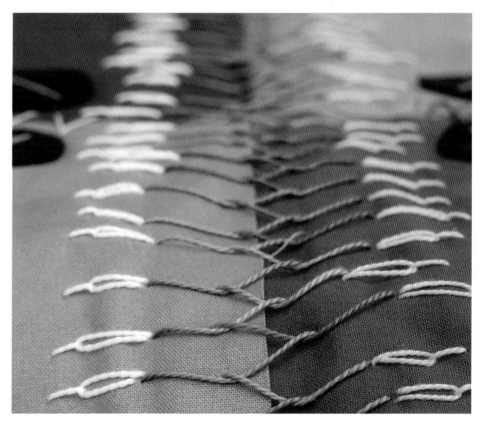

FIGURE [E]

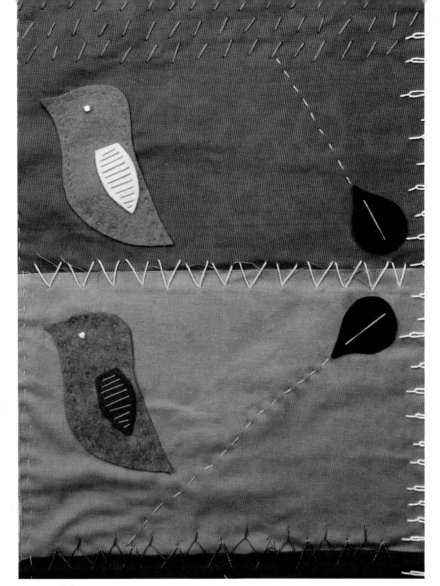

FIGURE [F]

Scan and print the Doodle Love Raindrop templates per the instructions on page 126. With a fabric marking pen, trace it onto a single color of felt eight times. Arrange the fabric raindrops so that they are in the corner of a rectangle. Add to the quilt with a long straight stitch down the center of the raindrop and continue the straight stitch onto the printed fabric until it reaches another stitched area.

Repeat step 4 to trace the Doodle Love Bird template onto different pieces of felt to make a total of eight birds. Attach the wing pieces to the birds using a series of straight stitches. Attach the birds to the quilt at the edges of the rectangles (FIGURE F).

6

Complete the quilt by stitching a running stitch (see page 32) around the edges to secure the fabric backing and the quilt top together.

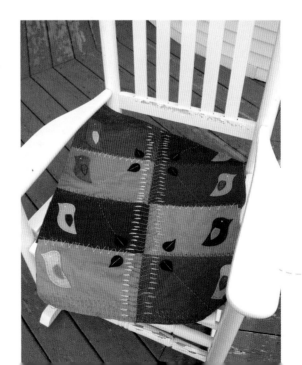

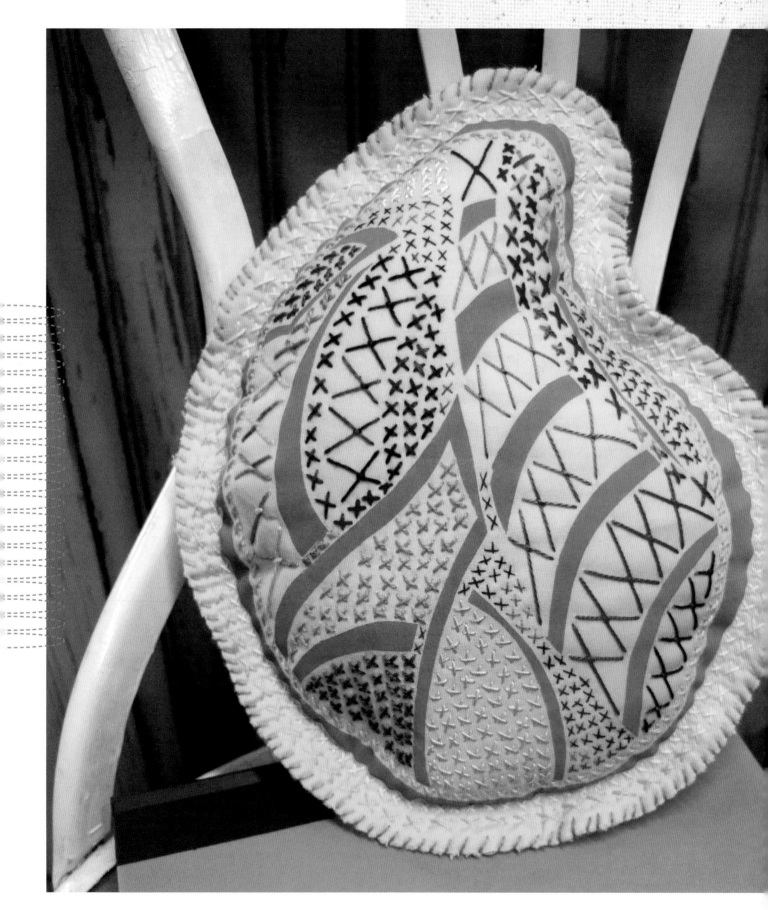

Technicolor Begonia Cushion

This quirky little cushion draws its inspiration from the free spirit of the begonia plant. My affection for these plants is based hugely on their refusal to conform. They grow in whatever direction they like, as big as they want, and flower when they choose to. They march to the beat of their own drummer.

The pattern for this cushion was created in "Creating Your Own Pattern for Stitching" (see page 48). Its demure size allows you to toss it in your bag and carry it with you for stitching in those odd moments. The only stitch I used on this project was the X stitch, a nod to the world of cross-stitch patterns, which is likely to be the first exposure to hand stitching most of us experience. Varying the size of the stitch and using various threads (cotton, wool, and silk) gives our little cushion a healthy dose of texture.

Last, I cut my cushion the shape of the leaf I designed. It makes it the perfect size for resting a book on while you're reading or tucking behind your head when you're relaxing on the patio. (And besides, the world has enough square cushions, doesn't it?)

M/A/T/E/R/I/A/L/S

Scissors

Stenciled fabric made in *Creating Your Own Pattern for Stitching* (p. 48). You can use the template on page 131, or follow the steps on pages 48–53 to create your own.

Two 12" × 12" (30.5 × 30.5 cm) pieces of thick wool felt

Pins

Sizes 5, 8, and 12 embroidery thread in various colors and fiber contents

Size 20 chenille needle

Size 5 embroidery needle

Polyfill stuffing

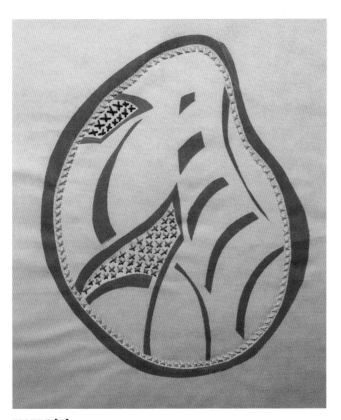

FIGURE [A]

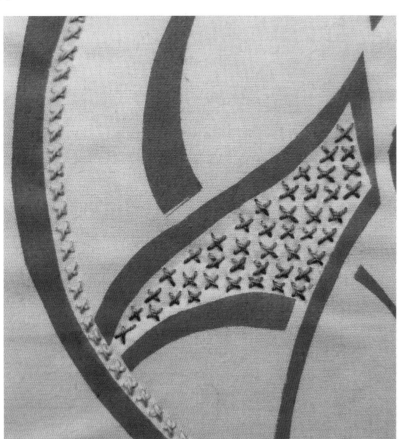

1

With scissors, trim your stenciled fabric to a 12" × 12" (30.5 × 30.5 cm) square. Lay it on top of a 12" × 12" (30.5 × 30.5 cm) piece of thick wool felt and pin it.

2

Using various threads and the appropriate needles, begin stitching by working a small X stitch (see page 28) between the inside border and the leaf veins. Then fill in the sections of the leaf with different colors and sizes of X stitches (FIGURE A).

3

After you have filled in the entire leaf, lay the stitched front right side up on top of the second piece of wool felt. Pin in place. Stitch two rows of Xs around the outer border to secure the back felt to the front. Leave a 2" to 3" (5 to 7.6 cm) opening along one side to allow for stuffing.

4

Trim the pillow to the shape of the leaf. Leave a generous ¼" (6.4 mm) border around the edge and don't trim the stuffing opening close. This will give you some extra material to hold on to while you stuff the pillow (FIGURE B).

5

Using the polyfill stuffing, stuff the cushion as much as you'd like. You can make a firm pillow or a soft one—it's totally up to you. When you're done, trim the extra material at the opening and add X stitches to complete the outer border.

6

Secure the edges by whip stitching the back and front together to create a solid outer seam.

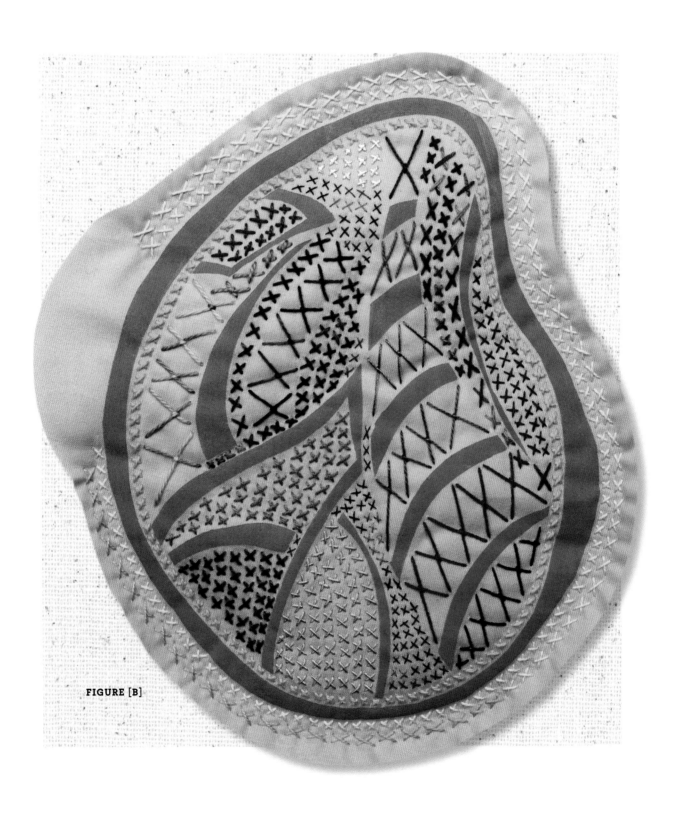

FIGURE [B]

Paper
PROJECTS

You may ask "Why would I want to stitch on *paper*?"
My answer would be, "Why wouldn't you?"
The surprise of thread on paper creates a fun pop
of the unusual. It can be the main focus of a project or
the perfect added touch to bring a project to life!

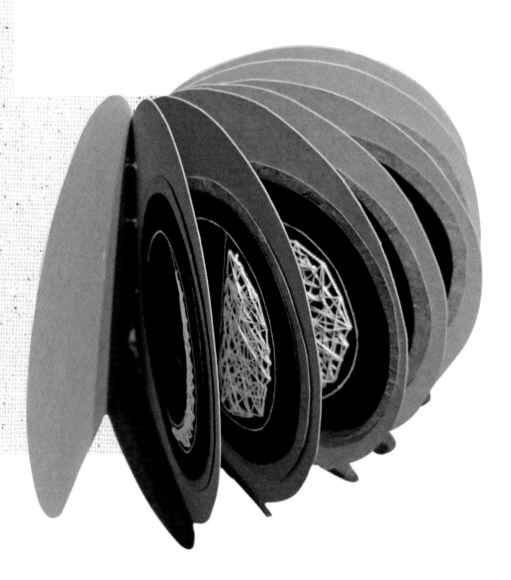

Stitched Botanical Note Card

Those days when I was a kid making cards for special occasions or loved ones still stick with me. It's a pleasure to both give and receive handmade items, and cards are a simple gesture that put a smile on everyone's face.

This note card elevates the scribble crayon cards we gave Mom for her birthday. We still get to indulge our love of coloring but by adding delicate stitching, we elevate this simple token of appreciation into a work of art.

M/A/T/E/R/I/A/L/S

Word-processing software

Scanner

Stitched Botanical Note Card template (p. 132)

Printer

Computer printable note cards or card stock that can be cut to in half so that the card measures 4¼" × 5½" (10.8 × 13.8 cm). You'll need two note cards or sheets of card stock; one will be left blank.

Markers

Six-stranded embroidery floss

Size 5 embroidery needle

Masking tape

1

Open up a blank document in word-processing software. Reduce the margins to zero on all edges. Scan the Stitched Botanical Note Card template into your computer, add it to the document, and stretch to fit the page.

2

Print the file onto the note card or card stock.

3

Color in areas of the card with markers (FIGURE A).

4

Pull one strand of yellow floss and one strand of orange floss or colors of your choosing. Add seed stitch (see page 28) in the corner motifs, using the techniques for adding holes to paper with an embroidery needle from page 25. Secure the tail with a piece of masking tape (FIGURE B).

5

Stitch a single running stitch (see page 32) down the center of each leaf in a contrasting color (FIGURE C).

6

Fold the card in half and stitch the center of the flower with feather stitch (see page 38) and two strands of magenta floss. Turn the card 180 degrees when you reach the end of a row and stitch it in the opposite direction. This will add interest to the pattern and prevent you from you from having to secure multiple start and stop threads. Use X stitch (see page 28) in the center of the half circles (FIGURE D).

FIGURE [A]

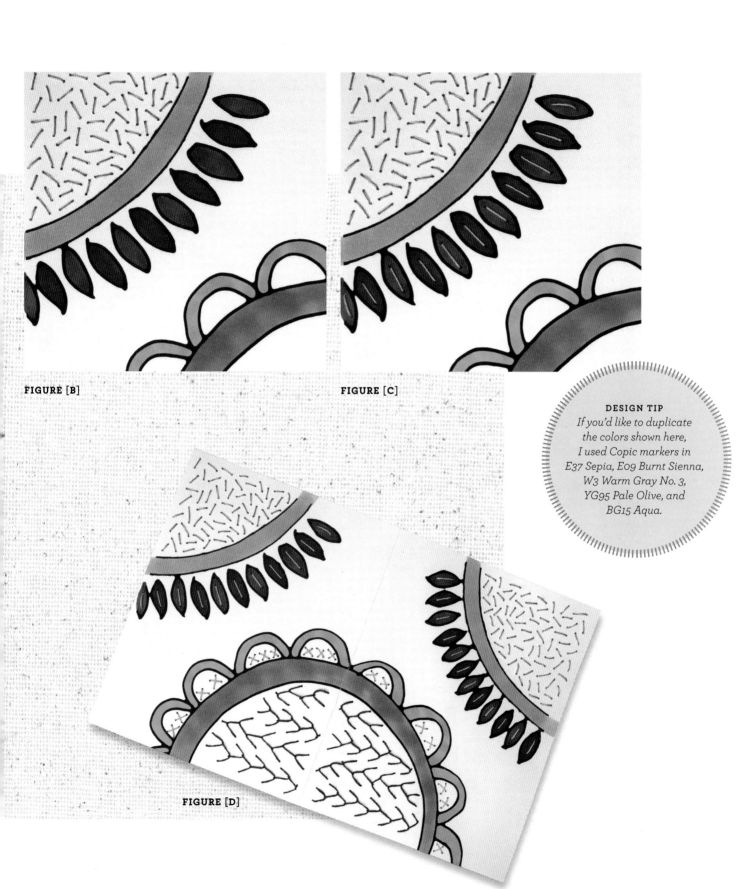

FIGURE [B]

FIGURE [C]

DESIGN TIP
*If you'd like to duplicate
the colors shown here,
I used Copic markers in
E37 Sepia, E09 Burnt Sienna,
W3 Warm Gray No. 3,
YG95 Pale Olive, and
BG15 Aqua.*

FIGURE [D]

Stamped and Stitched Book Ribbon

As a writer, I think there is nothing prettier in the world than crisp black letters marching across a white page. There's something magical about knowing these little shapes create ideas, display the author's imagination so clearly, and teach.

M/A/T/E/R/I/A/L/S

Black permanent marker

1" × 4" (2.5 × 10.2 cm) rubber stamp carving block

Stamp-carving tool or craft knife blade

Old book

Ruler

Ink pad

Paper clips

Size 8 perle cotton in three colors

Size 5 embroidery needle

Wooden spool (optional)

Low-tack masking tape (optional)

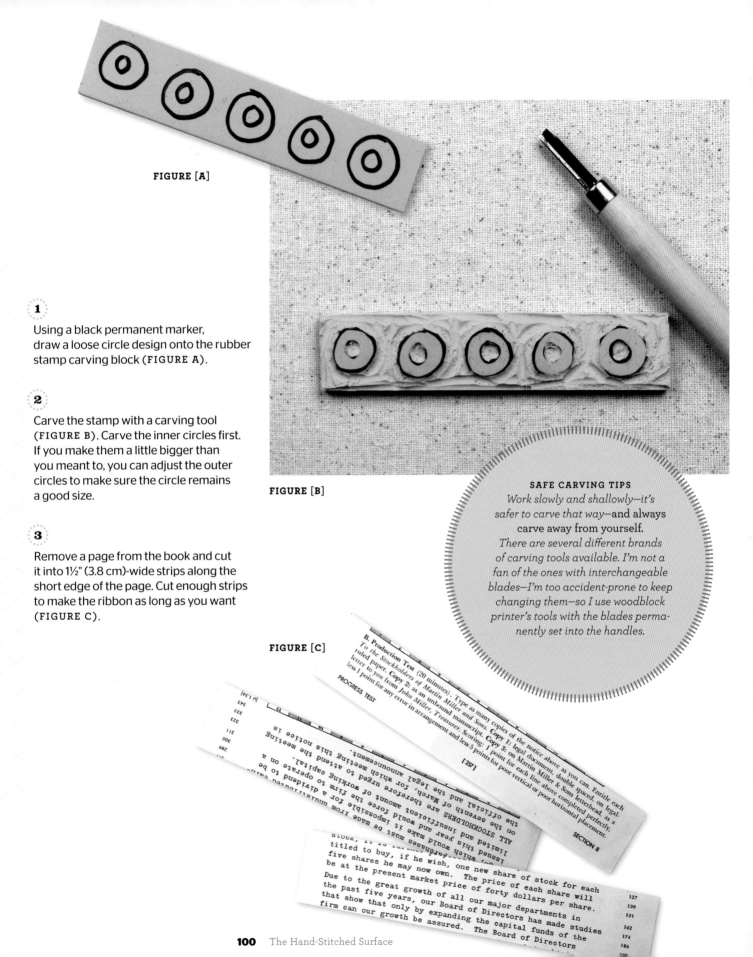

FIGURE [A]

1

Using a black permanent marker, draw a loose circle design onto the rubber stamp carving block (FIGURE A).

2

Carve the stamp with a carving tool (FIGURE B). Carve the inner circles first. If you make them a little bigger than you meant to, you can adjust the outer circles to make sure the circle remains a good size.

3

Remove a page from the book and cut it into 1½" (3.8 cm)-wide strips along the short edge of the page. Cut enough strips to make the ribbon as long as you want (FIGURE C).

FIGURE [B]

FIGURE [C]

SAFE CARVING TIPS
Work slowly and shallowly—it's safer to carve that way—and always carve away from yourself.
There are several different brands of carving tools available. I'm not a fan of the ones with interchangeable blades—I'm too accident-prone to keep changing them—so I use woodblock printer's tools with the blades permanently set into the handles.

4

Ink your stamp and stamp the circles down the center of each strip (FIGURE D).

5

Line up the strips by placing the first stamped circle on one strip on top of the last stamped circle on the previous strip (FIGURE E).

6

Secure the two pieces together using a paper clip for stitching (FIGURE F).

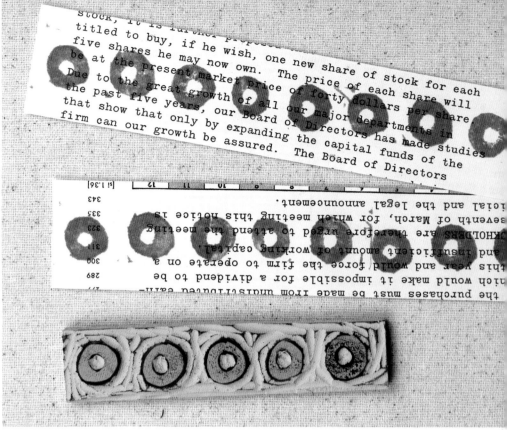
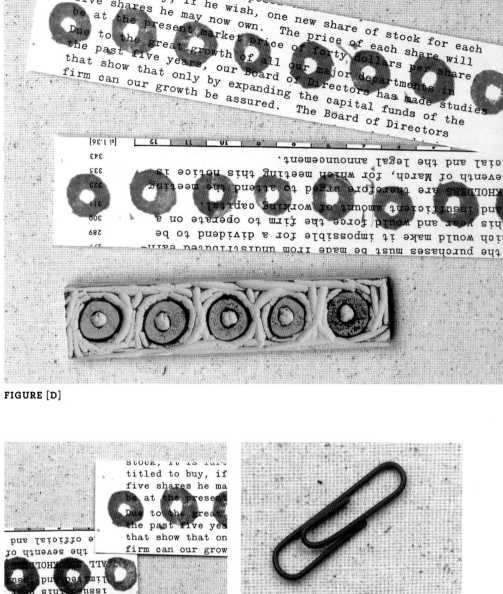

FIGURE [D]

TECHNIQUE TIP
It's much easier to work with only one paper clip joint at a time. Add one strip on at a time as you stitch.

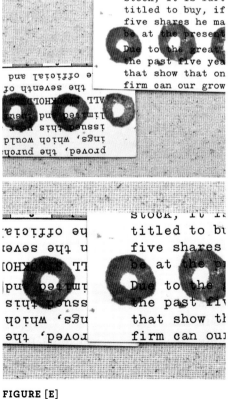

FIGURE [E]

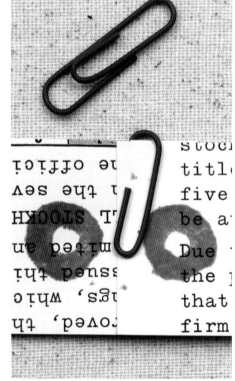

FIGURE [F]

7

Using a running stitch (see page 32), stitch over and under the stamped circle design to create a boundary for the edge stitching. Running stitch is shown in red thread in Figure G.

8

Using a loose satin stitch (see page 32), stitch along one edge of the paper ribbon. Work close to the edge of the paper, up to the edge of the circle stitching or stamped image.

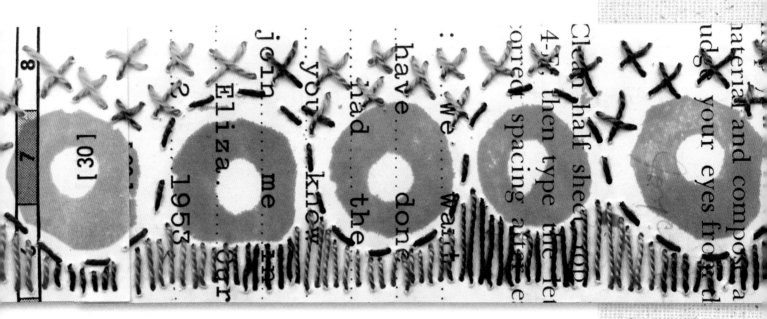

FIGURE [G]

9

Using X stitches (see page 28), stitch along the other edge of the paper ribbon. Work close to the edge of the paper, up to the edge of the circle stitching or stamped image (FIGURE G). X stitching is shown in green thread.

10

To display your ribbon on a spool, attach one end to the spool using low-tack masking tape. Loosely wind around the spool. Cut a length of thread and pass it through the center hole of the spool, tying a bow in the center to act as a loose hold on the spool.

To use your ribbon in a project, attach it with double-sided tape rather than liquid glue.

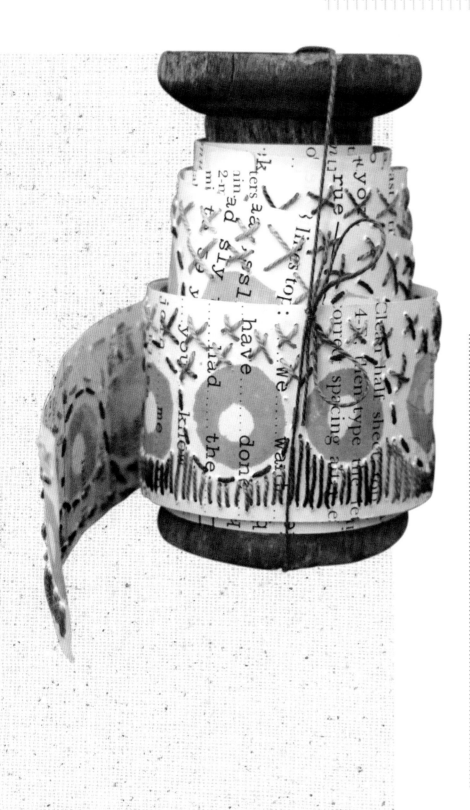

Repurposing Old Books

I have a special affection for older books. Although I started out a little conflicted over cutting them up and using them in art projects, I've realized that giving them a new life offers me the chance to admire them in a new light.

This paper ribbon is made from strips of an old typing-instruction manual. It's about 1 yard (91 cm) long, but can be created for any length you like. Use them in your scrapbooks, art journals, and greeting cards, or do what I do—set it on a shelf and admire it.

Embellished Photos

My brother takes the most fantastic photos. His eye for detail never ceases to inspire me. Often when I view his photography, I find myself wondering about the story behind them. There always seems to be some kind of secret lurking.

Stitching on photographs is a perfect way to convey a story. Take two photos that you feel create a dialogue and unify them with stitching. The stitches added here are simpler and less dense than some of the other projects in the book. But it's a good example of how hand stitching can be the background element that ties the entire project together.

M/A/T/E/R/I/A/L/S

2 photographs to stitch on (I used 4" × 4" [10.2 × 10.2 cm] photos printed at Snapfish.com, so my blank card is sized to suit those. If you use different size photos, change the size of the blank card as needed.)

4½" × 6" (11.5 × 15.2 cm) blank card

Double-sided tape

Size 5 embroidery thread

Size 20 chenille needle

Background paper (optional)

1

Choose two photos that tell a story. Seek out any additional ephemera that might complement them (FIGURE A).

2

Attach the elements to the blank card using double-sided tape. Try not to add tape to areas where you will be stitching (FIGURE B).

3

Add stitching that conveys the message between the two photos. For example, I stitched little pink hearts around Kewpie by overlapping two chain stitches (see page 36). The long running stitches (see page 32) and oversized French knots (see page 38) on top of the phone indicate eager ringing. All the other stitching helps add whimsy to the story (FIGURE C).

4

When done, secure any loose photo edges with additional double-sided tape (FIGURE D). If the exposed threads on the back bother you, cover them with additional paper.

FIGURE [A]

FIGURE [B]

TECHNIQUE TIP
I used the needle I was stitching with to poke the holes from the front of the photo.

FIGURE [C]

Using Photos for Stitching

Never use photos without permission; it's not okay to copy images off of the internet and have them printed to use in a project. Always ask first. Remember that photography is art, too, and you'd want others to ask you before using your work in their project.

The story for my photos was inspired by the Kewpie doll holding the phone. She looks so excited, and I imagine her calling someone she has a crush on. The other photo is black and white, lending a little mystery as to whom she is courting. I tore some strips of paper out of an old phone book to add interest to the background. I attached all the pieces to a blank card, which can stand up and be displayed immediately.

When deciding on a photo story, it doesn't have to be literal. It could also be a color story or a single photo with the added special touch of hand stitching.

FIGURE [D]

Paper Succulent Garden

I am a plant hoarder and, yes, I declare that loud and proud. My obsession revolves around a few specific types of plants, and succulents and cacti head up the pack by a landslide. I first discovered these little wonders when I visited a local nursery, Graye's Greenhouse. Rows and rows of these bizarre little wonders of nature pack their shelves, constantly amazing me with their beauty.

Our little paper garden takes some liberties in the color and marking department. Succulents and cacti aren't just green; they blush purples and reds when exposed to high levels of sunlight and often come in various shades of blue.

The beauty of this little garden is that it needs no care. Just stitch it up and enjoy it wherever your surroundings could use a good dose of color and nature.

M/A/T/E/R/I/A/L/S

Paper Succulent Garden templates (pp. 134–135)

Scissors or craft knife and cutting mat

Medium-weight card stock in the following colors: light green, medium green, light blue, brown, orange, light purple, and medium red

Size 8 embroidery thread in various colors

Size 20 Chenille needle

Masking tape

Box to attach plants to (or you may set them in a pot)

Craft glue

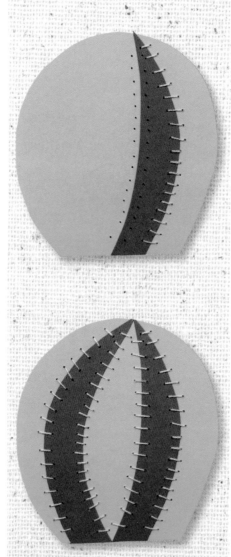

FIGURE [A]

1

Scan and print the templates per the instructions on page 126. Beginning with the Cactus template, trace the outer shape onto the light green paper and cut it out.

Cut the two sections of the Cactus template with hatch marks away from the whole and trace those onto the medium green paper. Cut them out.

Attach the medium green paper to the light green paper using yellow embroidery thread, using the chenille needle to poke the holes through the paper. Secure the thread starts and ends with tape on the back of the paper (FIGURE A).

2

Repeat the same process for the Aloe template using light blue and light green paper. Add more stitching to outline the leaves (FIGURE B).

FIGURE [B]

3

Repeat the same process for the Lithops template, using brown and orange paper and adding stitching for texture and interest (FIGURE C).

4

Repeat the same process for the Sedum template, using light purple and medium red paper. Add stitching details to each for interest and texture (FIGURE D).

5

After creating all of the succulents, attach them to a box with craft glue. Attach the sedum first, then the aloe and cactus, and finally the lithops. Allow the glue to dry between each layer (FIGURE E).

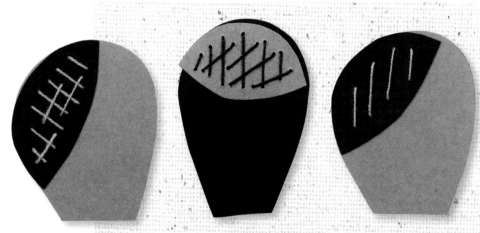

FIGURE [C]

FIGURE [D]

FIGURE [E]

Mended-Paper Painting

Mending is about as utilitarian as stitching can get. Though it technically isn't stitching, having its roots planted more in the weaving camp, it's something that I admire for many reasons. The first is that it's used to repair items. There is immense beauty in items that are worn through, and the quest to preserve them by mending commands great respect. The other is that mending presents a unique opportunity for design and color.

Although mending immediately brings to mind worn-out jeans or a jacket with a hole in the elbow, we're going to give it a twist and apply it to a paper project. This is slow, careful work, but the texture and density of the resulting weaving is addictive. It's also an opportunity to use fancy paper in the window of the weaving area, giving us a chance to feature the unusual.

M/A/T/E/R/I/A/L/S

Mended-Paper Painting template (p. 133)

Craft knife

Ruler

Cutting mat

Size 22 chenille embroidery needle

8½" × 11" (21.6 × 28 cm) piece of chipboard

8½" × 11" (21.6 × 28 cm) piece of white textured paper

Masking tape

2 binder clips

4 colors of size 5 perle embroidery thread—two dark, one light, and one contrasting

8" × 8" (20.3 × 20.3 cm) wood artist panel

Craft glue

1

Scan and print out the templates per the instructions on page 126. Cut out the circle area that is crosshatched using a craft knife and ruler on a cutting mat. Cut out the square shape. Using a size 22 chenille needle, poke holes in each dot.

2

Cut the chipboard into four 4" (10.2 cm) squares and the white paper into four 3½" (8.9 cm) squares. Trace the circle from the template onto each piece of chipboard and cut out (FIGURE A).

3

On one side of the chipboard (it doesn't matter which side), center the white paper over the cutout opening and secure with masking tape (FIGURE B).

4

Place the template on the front of the chipboard/white paper square and secure it with two binder clips. Using the embroidery needle, follow the template as a guide to poke holes through the chipboard/white paper square (FIGURE C).

FIGURE [A]

FIGURE [B]

FIGURE [C]

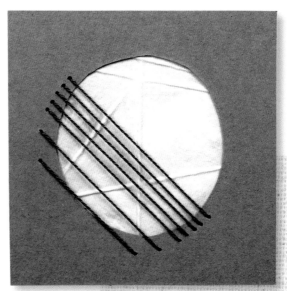

5

Thread the needle with size 5 dark thread and add long threads to act as the base for the weaving. Pull firmly to keep taut. After you've pulled the thread through each of the prepunched holes, punch another hole between each of the template holes, eyeballing the distance. Add another set of threads to create a tighter weaving platform (FIGURE D).

6

Thread the needle with light thread and, beginning close to the darker thread, but in the opposite direction, poke a hole with the needle (again, estimating the distance) and bring the thread to the top. Weave the lighter thread over and under the darker thread. Go back down through the chipboard on the opposite end of the circle (FIGURE E).

7

With the second darker color, add another layer of weaving near the existing dark-thread template holes. Add holes just outside the original set. Don't poke the new holes too close to the old ones (FIGURE F).

8

Repeat step 7 in the opposite direction with the contrasting color thread to complete the weaving.

9

Arrange the completed woven squares so that the dark areas are in the center. Attach to the wood panel with craft glue.

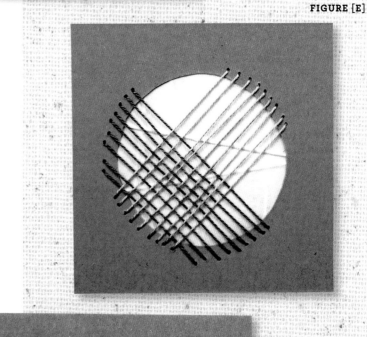

FIGURE [E]

FIGURE [F]

Origami Candy Catcher

When you've had a long day, nothing picks up your spirits better than a little sweet treat. Candy is an instant happiness maker. And placing it in a cute little handmade holder makes it all the more special.

These petite Origami Candy Catchers are just the ticket to cheer up a friend, create unique party favors, or even add some edible home décor to one of your spaces!

M/A/T/E/R/I/A/L/S

Tracing paper

Origami Candy Catcher template (p. 136)

Masking tape

No. 2 pencil

4" × 5" (10.2 × 12.7 cm) rubber stamp carving block

Scissors

Cutting mat

U-shaped stamp carving tool

Scrap paper

Ink pad

6" × 6" (15.2 × 15.2 cm) origami paper in multiple colors

Size 5 or 8 perle cotton. (This is a great project to show off your variegated threads.)

Size 5 embroidery needle. (This size is a tight fit for the perle cotton, but we want to limit the size of the holes in the paper. Plus, with the thread rose stitch, the needle doesn't pass through the paper that many times.)

FIGURE [A]

1

Place tracing paper on top of the template and tape the corners down. Trace with a pencil. On the tracing paper, draw hatch lines to show the black parts of the pattern (FIGURE A).

2

Place the tracing paper pencil-side down on the carving block. To transfer the design to the block, hold the paper firmly in place and apply pressure as you run the scissor handles' smooth edge across the paper (FIGURE B).

3

Working on a cutting mat with the carving tool, slowly carve all of the spaces of the block that *don't* have hatch marks. Don't cut deeply. You can always carve more away if you feel there are too many carving marks showing up in your print, but you can't put back a big chunk once you've hacked it out. (See page 100 for detailed information on carving.) When you're finished, do a test print on a scrap of paper to see whether there are any areas where you might like to carve more.

FIGURE [B]

4

Fold the origami paper according to the diagram (FIGURE C). Step 1 is accomplished by folding the paper in half, point to point, to form a triangle. *In pencil,* lightly draw an "X" on one of the corners of the closed end to mark the side of the paper that will be stamped.

5

Make sure the creases on your folded candy catcher are crisp. Unfold and place it X side up.

6

Ink your stamp and stamp one half of the paper, lining up the edges of the stamp with the creases of the triangles at the top and bottom (FIGURE D).

7

Re-ink the stamp and then stamp the other half of the paper (FIGURE E).

8

Allow the ink to dry and then refold the candy catcher (FIGURE F).

9

Stitch a thread rose (see page 40) on each of the triangle flaps. Add leaves by stitching lazy daisy stitches (see page 34) in green.

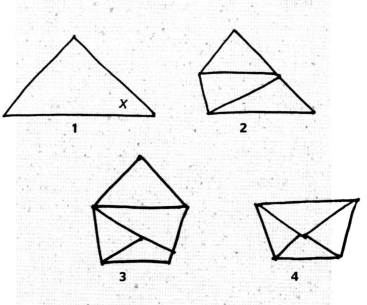

FIGURE [C]

FIGURE [D]

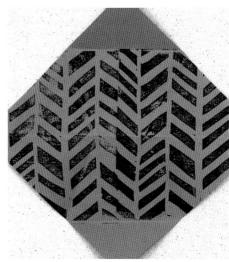

FIGURE [E]

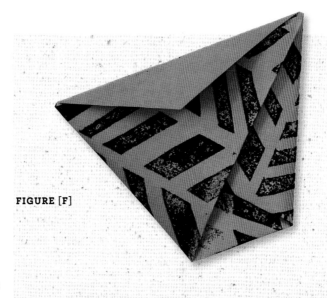

FIGURE [F]

Moon Phase Calendar

The moon is a constant source of mystery and inspiration, always being nothing but beautiful at every phase. I've always felt like it's keeping a watchful eye on everyone down here, making sure we are safe and happy.

This project has several steps and components, as it's a combination of calendar, book, and stacked loose satin stitching. We are making a calendar that has no expiration date and honors our ever-watchful friend.

M/A/T/E/R/I/A/L/S

Moon Phase Calendar templates A–G and Hole template (pp. 137–139)

Craft knife

Cutting mat

White gel pen

Four 8½" × 11" (21.6 × 28 cm) sheets of medium-weight black card stock

Four 8½" × 11" (21.6 × 28 cm) sheets of medium-gray paper

Four 8½" × 11" (21.6 × 28 cm) sheets of chipboard

Scissors

Screw punch with ¹⁄₁₆" (1.5 mm) tip or size 22 chenille needle

Embroidery thread in the following colors and sizes: size 8 white, size 8 ecru, and white floss

Size 5 embroidery needle

Masking tape

2 binder clips

⅛" (3 mm) hole punch

Double-sided tape

Embroidery thread in a variety of colors to tie the book together

Beads and various embellishments (optional)

1

Scan and print the templates per the instructions on page 126. Cut them out with a craft knife on a cutting mat. On templates A–D, cut out the hatched areas inside the circles. You're only cutting out the hatched areas to make the templates, not on the card stock used for the moon.

2

Using a white gel pen, trace the inner and outer circles of template A onto the black card stock a total of eight times. Cut out each circle around the edge of the outer circle.

3

Set aside two of the circles from step 2 to use for the Full Moon and New Moon pages.

4

Place template B on top of one of the circles of black card stock from step 2 and trace the shape in the cutout. Do this to make two circles to use for the First Quarter and Last Quarter pages.

5

Repeat step 4 using templates C and D. Template C pages are for the Waxing Gibbous and Waning Gibbous. Template D pages are for the Waxing Crescent and Waning Crescent (FIGURE A).

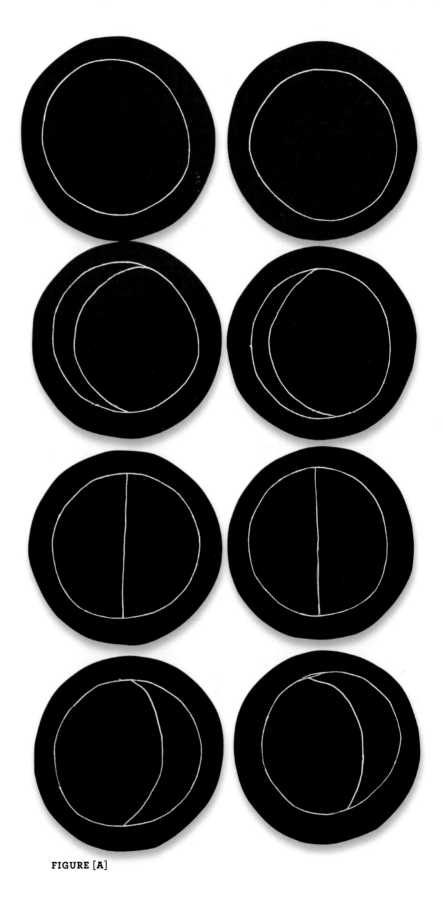

FIGURE [A]

6

Trace template E onto the gray paper eight times and cut out.

7

Trace template F onto the chipboard eight times and cut out.

8

Using the ⅟₁₆" (1.5 mm) tip on the screw punch, randomly punch holes in the area that is shown crosshatched on each Moon Phase template. Leave space between each punch. Don't punch any holes on the New Moon phase (FIGURE B).

9

Using size 8 white perle cotton and an embroidery needle, create running stitches (see page 32) between the holes. Allow the pattern to be random. This layer does not need to be dense (FIGURE C).

10

Add a second layer of random straight stitching using the size 8 ecru thread. Add the final layer of random straight stitching with a single thread of white floss (FIGURE D).

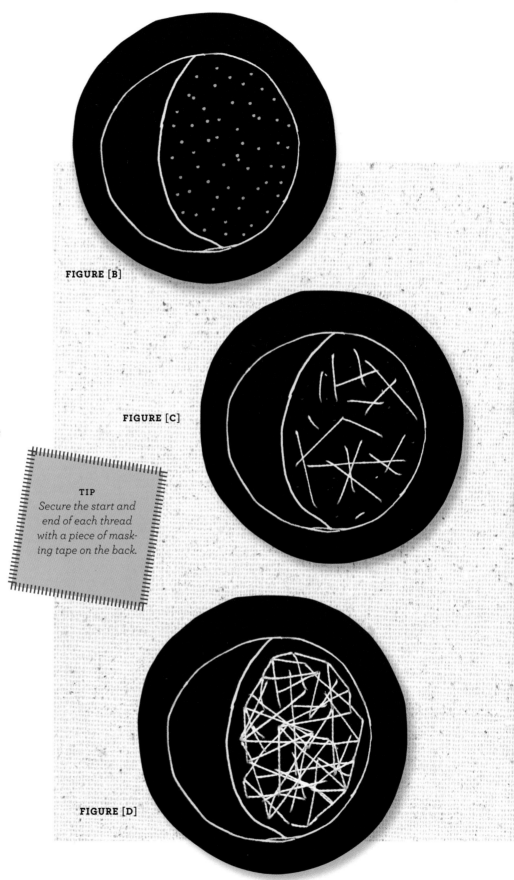

FIGURE [B]

FIGURE [C]

TIP
Secure the start and end of each thread with a piece of masking tape on the back.

FIGURE [D]

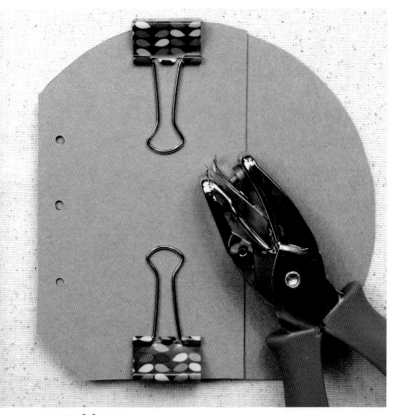

FIGURE [E]

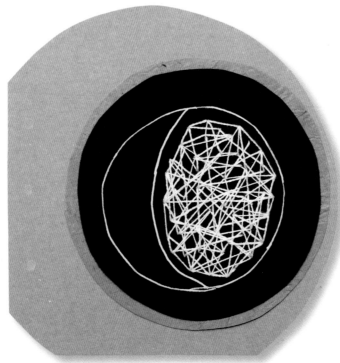

FIGURE [F]

Line up the Hole template at the edge of each chipboard page. Secure with binder clips so it doesn't move. Trace the holes with a pencil. Remove the template and use the hole punch to punch out the holes (FIGURE E).

12

Assemble the moon phases onto each page in the following order:

Using double-sided tape, secure the stitched black card stock to the gray paper (FIGURE F).

Using double-sided tape, secure the completed moon to the chipboard page, lining it up about ¾" (1.9 cm) from the edge where the holes were punched. Be sure to position them according to the phases, as shown (FIGURE G).

13

Using embroidery floss in a variety of weights, thread them through the holes and tie loosely. Add any extra embellishments to them (FIGURES H, I).

FIGURE [G]

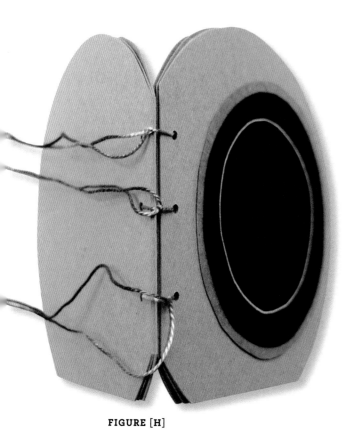

FIGURE [H]

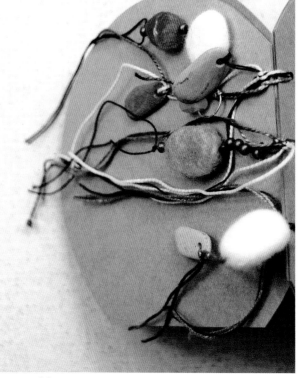

FIGURE [I]

TEMPLATES

The following templates provide the framework for your stitching. They are here to help you get started—feel free to explore and fill in with whatever stitch moves you!

To use the templates, scan and print them or download them from **http://smudgedesignstudio.com** or **www.quartoknows.com/page/hand-stitch**. Print all at 100 percent, except for the Technicolor Begonia Cushion, page 131, which should be enlarged to 115 percent before printing.

Boho Collage
Coasters

See project on pages 64–67.

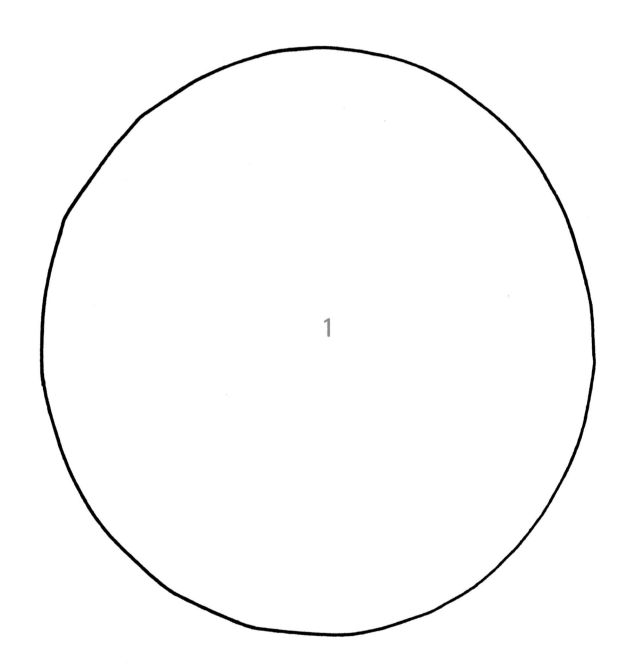

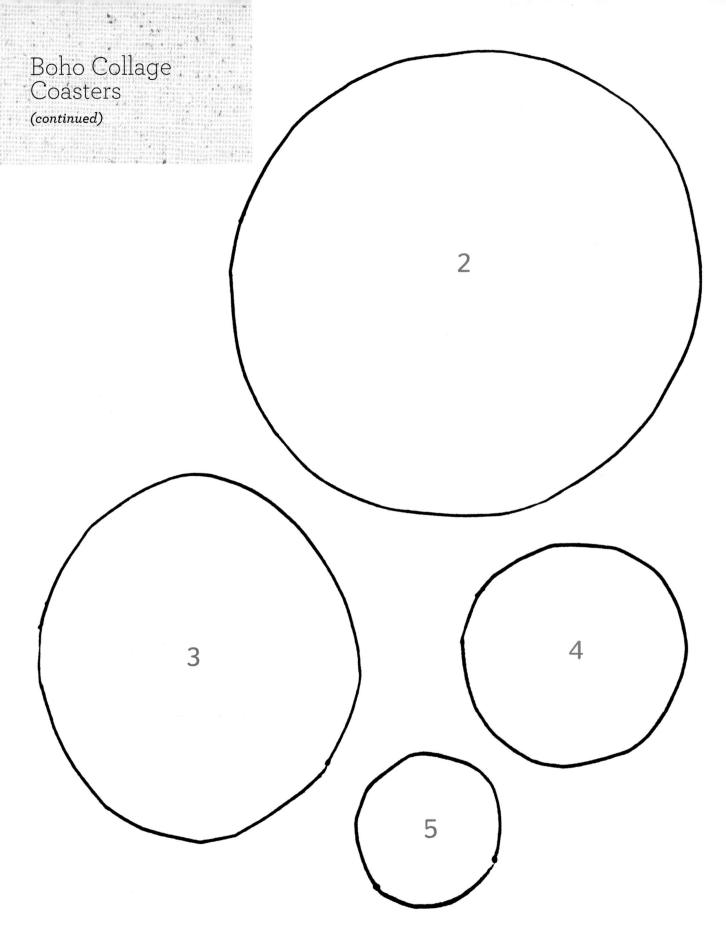

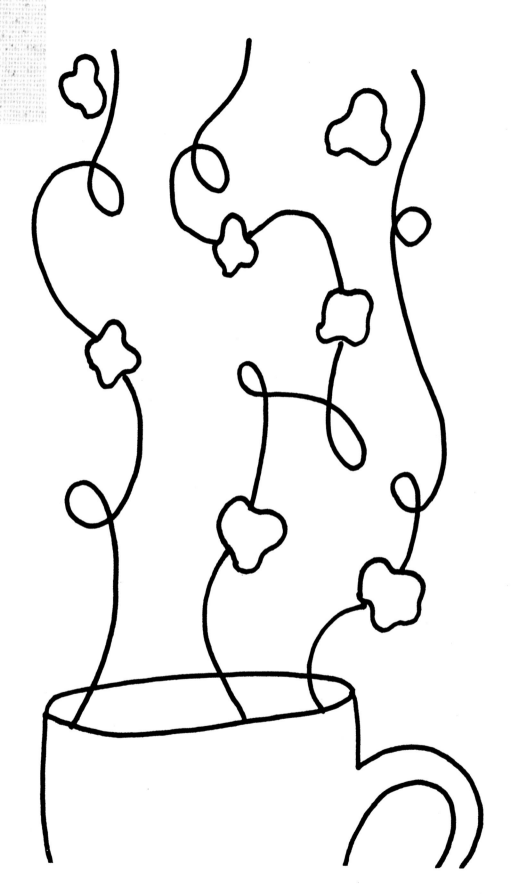

Color-Wedge
Stitched Sampler

See project on pages 78–81.

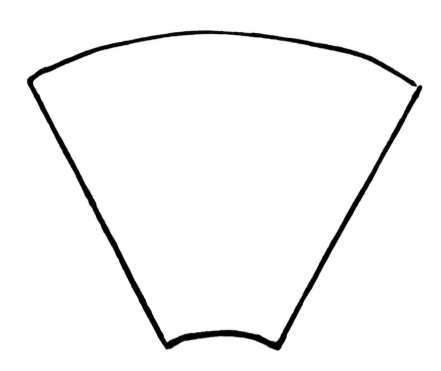

Doodle Love
Lap Quilt

See project on pages 82–87.

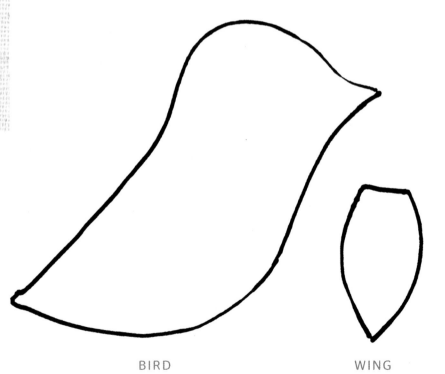

RAINDROP

BIRD

WING

Technicolor Begonia Cushion

See project on pages 88–91.
Enlarge template to 115 percent
before printing.

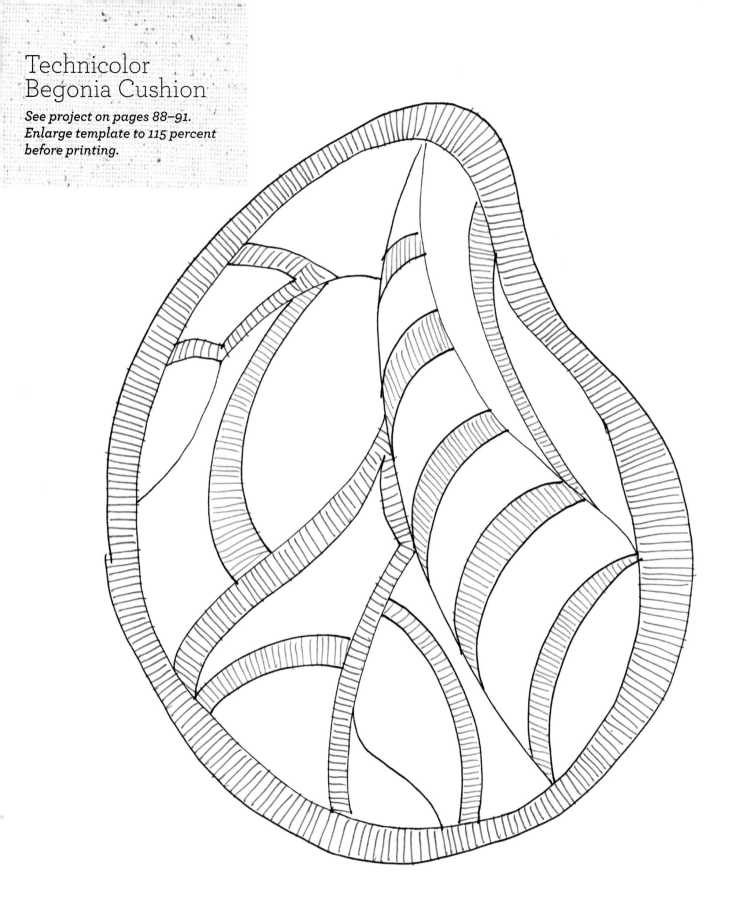

Mended-Paper
Painting

See project on pages 112–115.

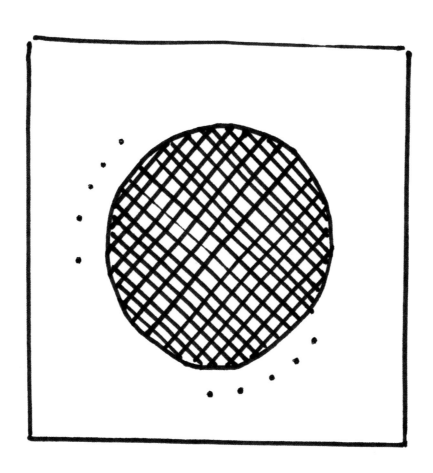

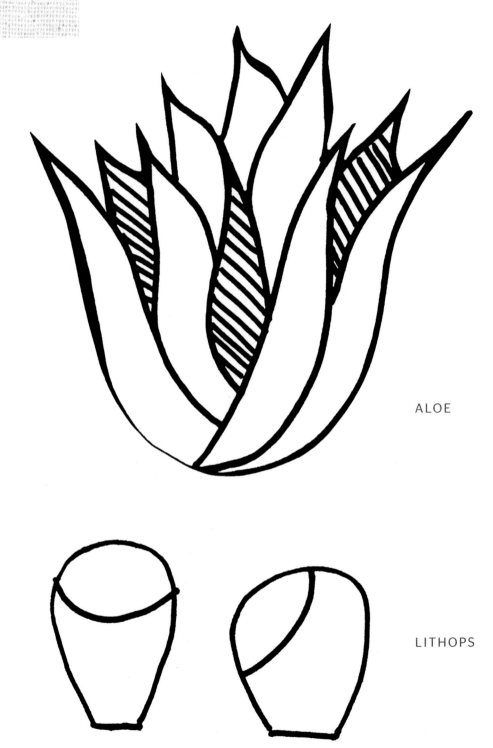

ALOE

LITHOPS

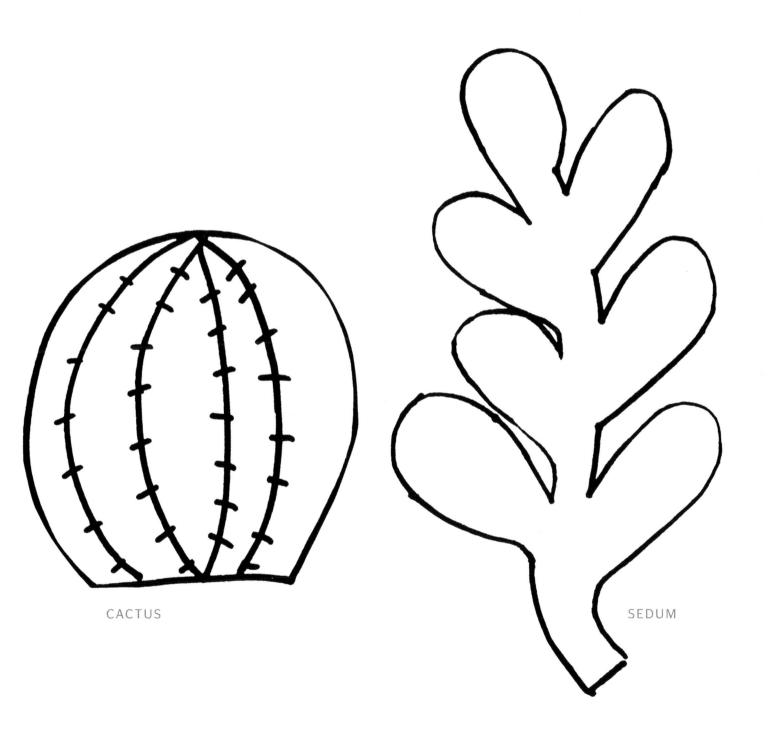

CACTUS

SEDUM

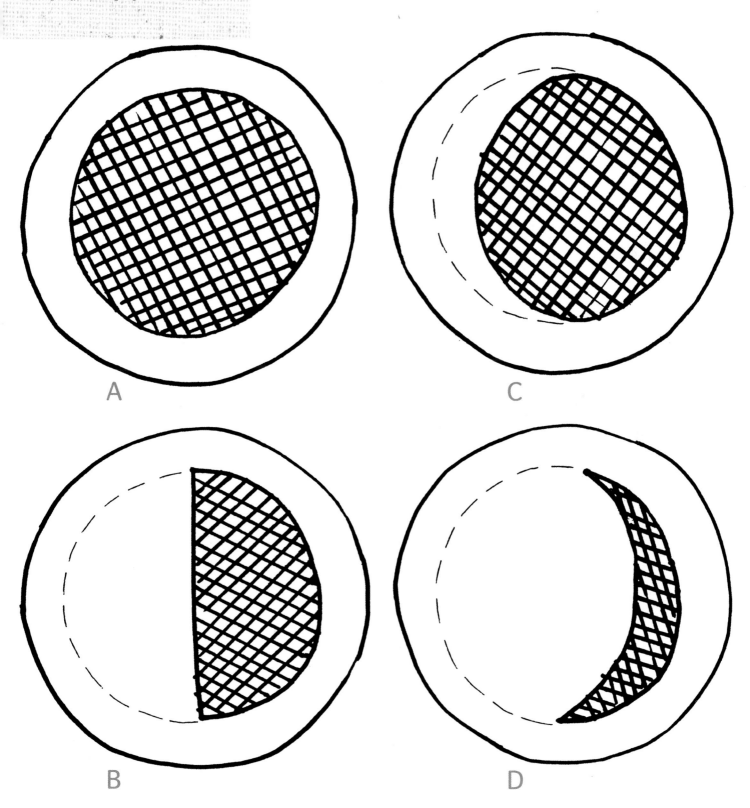

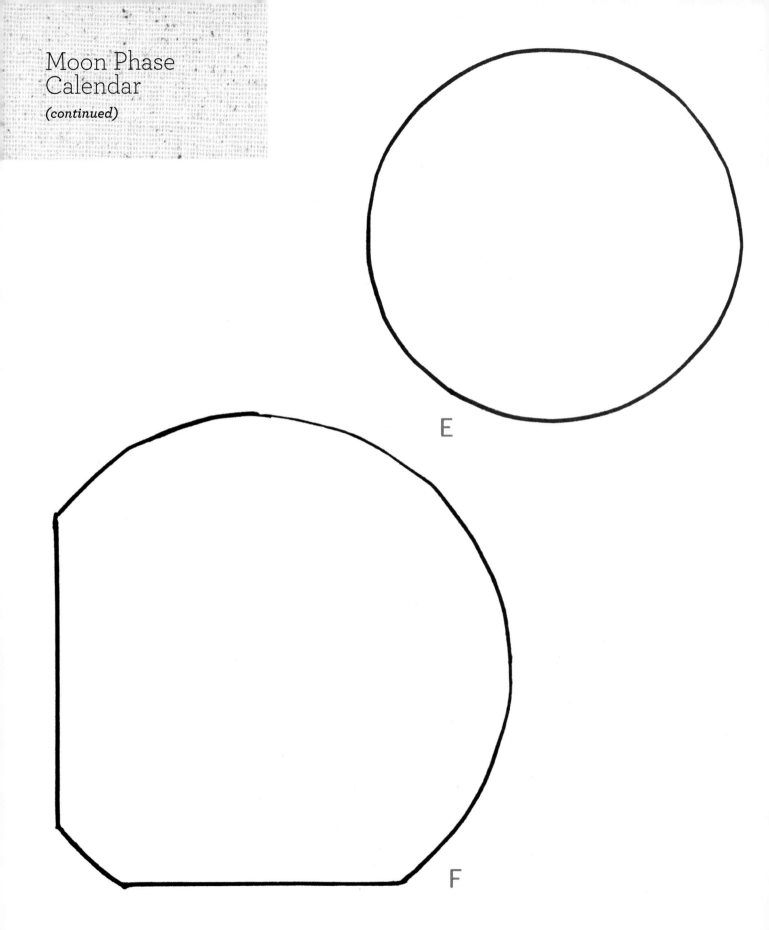

E

F

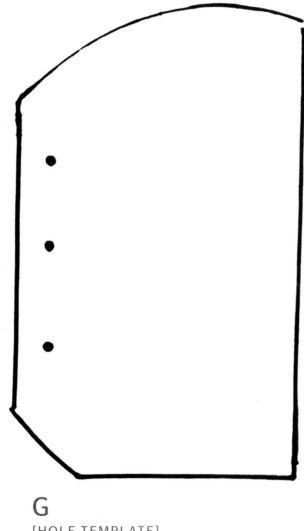

G
[HOLE TEMPLATE]

About the Author

Lynn Krawczyk is a mixed-media artist living in Michigan. Her work focuses on creating layers of color and pattern through original hand-printed fabric and stitching. She has written more than forty magazine articles, teaches through DVDs and online classes, believes that art will heal the world, and drinks coffee like it's going out of style.

Visit her at www.SmudgedDesignStudio.com

Acknowledgments

Books are never a solitary effort. From the idea to the layout to holding the finished project in your hand, there is an incredible amount of magic happening behind my scenes.

I want to thank Quarto for giving me the space to stitch like a madwoman and design the projects that speak to me. I also want to thank the editors and designers who have toiled to take what my creative side produced and organize it into a beautiful format. You are wonderful, Joy and Cara!

I'd also like to thank the art director, Anne, and designer Timothy for wrangling all my photos and words into the awesome arrangement you now are holding in your hands.

I'd also like to thank my mom for her unending support, my crazy dog Carter for his unending supervision in the studio, and all the local business owners who let me drag my finished projects around and use their wonderful spaces as backdrops for the photos.

And last, I'd like to thank my stitching idols—Allie Aller, Mark Lipinski, Judith Baker Montano, Dorothy Caldwell, and Lorie Hancock McCown. You all inspire me to keep needle and thread at hand and keep pushing the boundaries of what stitch can be.

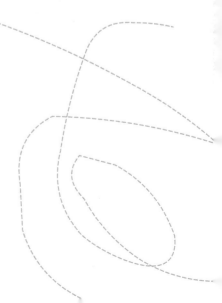

Resources

General Stitching and Crafts Supplies

Hobby Lobby Arts & Crafts Stores
www.hobbylobby.com

Jo-Ann Fabric and Craft Stores
www.joann.com

Michaels Arts & Crafts
www.michaels.com

Thread Resources

Purl Soho www.purlsoho.com

eBay www.ebay.com

Etsy www.etsy.com.
You can find many sellers of hand-dyed thread as well as vintage threads on these sites.

DMC www.dmc.com, www.dmc-usa.com

Aurifil www.aurifil.com

Week's Dye Works
www.weeksdyeworks.com

Treenway Silks
www.treenwaysilks.com

Colour Complements
www.colourcomplements.com

Wool Felt

Purl Soho www.purlsoho.com

Transdoodle Transfer Paper

Mistyfuse www.mistyfuse.com

Paper Sources

Hollander's www.hollanders.com

French Paper Co. www.frenchpaper.com

Paper Screw Punch and Book Board

Dick Blick Art Materials
www.dickblick.com

Cotton Quilting Fabric

e-Quilter www.equilter.com

Noncotton Fabric

Purl Soho www.purlsoho.com

Dyeable Fabric and Items

Dharma Trading Co.
www.dharmatrading.com

Indigo Dyeing Kit

Dharma Trading Co.
www.dharmatrading.com

Mixed-Media Paper, Wood Artist Panel, Tracing Paper, Stamp Carving Material, Carving Tools

Dick Blick Art Materials
www.dickblick.com

Index